SUCCEED
WITHOUT
BURNOUT

SUCCEED
WITHOUT
BURNOUT

*Proven strategies
to move your life from
Burnout to Balance*

Ben Kubassek

Eagle Press
Ayr, Ontario, Canada

Published in 1997 by
Eagle Press
R.R. #1, Ayr
Ontario, Canada
N0B 1E0

ISBN 0-9681538-0-1

Manufactured in the U.S.A. by BookCrafters

printing number

10 9 8 7 6 5 4 3 2

Cover Design: David Ziemann
Photography: John Mitchell
Editing: John Vardon
Cartoons: Fortunato Restagno

With love I dedicate this book to my wife, Elizabeth, and to my children, Krystal, Daniel, Joshua and Jonathan, who constantly inspire me to keep my life in balance.

I also dedicate this book to my parents, Julius & Theresa, who taught me as a child that *"What I was, was God's gift to me. What I would become, would be my gift to God."*

ACKNOWLEDGEMENTS

My life has truly been blest with abundance. I owe a debt of gratitude to my Creator, my family, my friends, and my mentors. I gratefully acknowledge and express my deep appreciation to the many wonderful people who have made this book possible:

To my mentors, whose writings, recordings and actions have blest and inspired me with the wisdom of the ages.

To my clients, colleagues, and team members whose synergy has empowered me to live beyond my own level of thinking.

To my associates at Missionary Ventures who have taught me the meaning of "meeting human needs through personal involvement." Knowing you has made me a more caring and compassionate person.

To my pastor, Lloyd Fretz, and my former pastors, Keith Gonyou, Ron Byers, and John Zuck for their spiritual influence on my life.

Most of all, to my family, whose loving support has made all the difference in the world. Thanks for reminding me daily which things come **first**.

Contents

Introduction

THE FARM

My road to burnout was distinctly my own. I was raised in the sheltered confines of a religious communal farm near Kitchener, Ontario. The Community Farm of the Brethren consisted of sixteen families living and working together, sharing all possessions and a modest lifestyle.

At the age of 21, with an 8th grade education and $2,000, I left the farm and went right into business with my oldest brother. Believing that I could do anything, have anything or be anything I wanted to be, I began to read every self-help book that I could get ahold of.

The businesses I started, became very successful. Within six years I had achieved every goal I had set for my entire life, goals that seemed unachievable even when I set them. The risks I had taken had paid off!

BURNOUT

Then one day, like a flash fire, burnout engulfed me, consuming my energy, my creativity, my positive mental attitude, my love for life, my vision for the future. It sent me spiraling into a state of depression that almost led to suicide. For six months, I lived through the hellish nightmare of burnout — physical, mental and spiritual.

In those lost months, I wanted someone to tell me that they had been through what I was going through and that, yes, I could and would get better. In the depths of my depression, I needed someone to wave a light at the top of this pit of depression I had fallen into, to show me the way out.

You may feel like you are teetering on the edge of a similar precipice, or have already fallen over the edge, or you may be living without a sense of purpose or direction. If so, I believe this book will give you hope, and inspire you to move from *burnout to balance*, from *mediocrity to excellence,* from *a mere existence* to the experience of *true living.*

A BETTER WAY TO LIVE

The reason for writing this book is simple: to share with you the principles for successful, balanced living. If applied consistently, these principles will act as a vaccine against the killer disease known as *burnout.* Referred to throughout this book as the balanced-life principles, they are the key to living a happy, healthy, love-filled and prosperous life - *the abundant life.*

I believe in living life to the hilt every day. Living the balanced-life principles will bring a sense of control to your life, a control that you never thought possible. If you are presently in the midst of burnout, the balanced-life principles will give you hope, the hope you need to recover. Once you have received hope, you are well on your way to recovery.

Action is always preceded by emotion, but emotion is always preceded by thought. My prayer is "That this book will first cause you to think about how you've been living your life and to reflect on the results you have received thus far; that it will bring you to a heightened sense of interior awareness; that the power of these words will inspire you as deeply as ever before; that the emotions stirred in you will cause you to take action that will improve your results in your future; that the results of the action you take will make you a better person at home, at work, at school and on the inside."

If you feel lost in the maze of life, this book can be your road map to inner peace, a sense of purpose, a sense of direction, a sense of balance and true happiness. I would be honored to be your guide, to lead the way along the path from burnout to balance. My mission is to serve you, by helping you to succeed without burnout.

– Ben Kubassek

What is this life all about?

In the 50s it was all about security and comfort.

In the 70s it was about wealth and status.

Today it is about balance.

CHAPTER — 1

THE BURNOUT EXPERIENCE

IT ALL BEGAN with a terrorizing grip of anxiety as we opened up the envelopes. The project was a big one—the biggest I had ever attempted: a 97-home residential subdivision, a far cry from the 16-unit apartment building and the 6 single-family homes I'd previously built, I'd already spent over $50,000 on engineering fees and had purchased the land. The bids we were opening that day would give me an early glimpse of how much money I stood to make on the deal.

But as the township clerk, my engineer and I sat opening envelope after envelope in the council chambers of the township offices that sunny April afternoon in 1987, the prospect of personal financial ruin lunged out at me, threatening to destroy all that I'd worked so hard for over the past five years. In that time I'd labored 80-hour weeks to build my small electrical contracting business into a group of companies involved in mechanical and electrical contracting, real estate development, home building, kitchen and bath retailing and renovations. It wasn't uncommon for me to put in long hours during the day and then return to work soon after dinner.

My evenings consisted of doing paper work, working on real estate deals, going out to estimate new electrical jobs or designing electrical control panels for customers till 10:00 or 11:00 p.m. My work habits weren't doing my marriage any good. My spouse and I seemed to be growing further and further apart. Despite that, and despite the ulcers that had developed in my stomach, the business was prospering beyond my wildest dreams.

Now, as we sat there tearing open the envelopes, bid after bid came in substantially higher than my engineers had estimated — 30 percent or more across the board. Site servicing alone was going to cost me $100,000 more than I'd expected. Getting the project together had already caused me a considerable amount of aggravation, but now it seemed that, far from making money, the deal was going to cost me everything I owned.

TERROR STRIKES

The funny thing was that it shouldn't have bothered me. Normally, I'd have said — So what? If I lose everything I've accumulated, I'll just turn around and make it all back in a couple of years. You can't lose experience. I'd always had the attitude that problems didn't exist, only challenges and opportunities. This time, however, was a different story. My heart palpitated wildly and waves of acute anxiety pulsed through me, a reaction unlike any other I'd ever experienced. I was scared, not only about the business but also by the unfamiliarity of fear itself.

That night in bed, my mind raced. As the guy who was always so positive, I could now find potential disasters lurking in almost every deal I was involved in. I was in a cold sweat, and if I got any more than an hour of sleep that night, I'd be surprised.

Morning failed to bring a respite. Normally, I'd have been out of bed by 6:30 am and out the door the by 7:00. On my way I'd grab a slice of toast and a coffee to propel me through the first part of my lengthy day. That morning however, I dreaded facing the day. Pulling myself off the bed, I made it as far as the couch before collapsing.

My wife Elizabeth wanted to know what was wrong but, I wasn't sure. I could only tell her about the anxieties that had coursed through my head during the night.

When I did summon up the energy to go to work, all I could do was walk into my office, shut the door and cry. I accomplished very little that morning, and when I went home for lunch, I broke down again. I ended up crawling into bed (after forcing myself to eat some lunch) and slept for a couple of hours.

EXHAUSTED

Although I didn't realize it at the time, the stress of the previous day had sent my life spinning out of control. My single-minded devotion to work, and the enormous number of hours I had poured into it, had pushed me to the brink of exhaustion. All it had taken was a crisis to send me plunging downward.

While I couldn't see it then, I can see it clearly now. Like many others, I was caught in the fast pace of late-20th century living. I was a machine moving at warp speed that never shut off, never enjoyed a let-up, until eventually breaking down.

As much as I desperately wanted the emotions of the first two days to fade, it seemed there was nothing I could do to alter my feelings. Worse still, they didn't disappear when I went to bed that night. They were there the next day ... and the next...and the next. From May to August I battled depression, anxiety, despair and lethargy. I went through the motions at work, and found myself having to build up energy for even the smallest of tasks.

A few people, like my brothers (three of whom also worked in the firm) and my construction superintendent, knew what I was going through; they helped bear the load of the business. Trying to camouflage my feelings in front of others, I faced a daily struggle to say the "good mornings," give the pep talks and be the team leader that everyone expects of the company president.

Today, I know that going to work ultimately aided in my recovery, but at the time I was constantly tempted to let the business slide.

It wasn't any easier at home. My kids wanted to play in the evenings, but after an exhausting day battling my emotions at the office, all I could do was lie on the couch and let my head spin. The noise they made irritated me greatly. They were just kids having fun, but I was in no mood for fun.

Everything was more difficult. Prying myself out of bed in the mornings was a chore. Obstacles that I would have steamrollered before now seemed insurmountable. I dreaded decisions that in the past I would have made virtually without thinking. The contractor's bids had ignited my burnout, but they weren't what was keeping my spirit in intensive care. In fact, the development deal had turned out much better than originally expected - I actually ended up making a considerable amount of money. The crisis surrounding the deal had merely brought to light much more fundamental problems.

SUICIDE

The worst times were when I was alone, especially on drives between work and home or between the office and a project, alone in the car with my thoughts, I would at times consider ending it all. My greatest fear was that I'd never get better. Furthermore, it was clear that the business success I'd counted on to give me happiness had ultimately brought me misery. Life had lost its meaning. Driving along the road, I often considered ramming my car into the closest solid object.

What I really longed for however, was someone to explain to me what I was going through, but it seemed nobody could. Well-meaning friends advised me to cut back on the stress in my life by selling the company. Some people urged me to stop being so negative and down in the dumps without realizing I had little control over how I felt. Even my doctor at first simply prescribed medication to calm my nerves and to help me sleep.

I had never thought about *burnout*. If I had heard the word, I hadn't known what people were talking about until, in September, my doctor informed me that what I was going through was total mental, physical and spiritual burnout. He ordered me to get away to Florida, telling me not to come back until I felt like myself again. The two and half weeks there helped me a great deal to relax and get my mind off the business.

Even more important was the fact that in the last few months, my experience with burnout had prompted me to re-examine my life. Fundamental changes were clearly in order, and the realizations I came to with the assistance of others, not only helped me pull out of my debilitating state, but have also made sure I didn't return. Among other things, these realizations have to do with achieving balance in life, dealing with stress and achieving goals in ways that avoid burnout.

By October 1987 my dark days were over, but my relationship with burnout was far from ended. To my surprise, I soon began meeting others with the same symptoms I had experienced. Once I had become attuned to the problem, I was astonished at how commonplace an affliction *burnout* is. At one point I had thought despairingly that I was the only one experiencing *burnout;* then I realized that many others were going through it as well—in differing degrees of severity.

Now, I regularly meet people in the midst of burnout or rushing headlong towards it. Often they don't even have to say a word; I can pick up the non-verbal clues. They force smiles, their lips have turned a whitish hue and their eye sockets are deepened. They're fidgety, can't seem to relax and usually are not grooming themselves as well as they used to. These are all telltale signs of a person headed for burnout. Having been there, as a burnout waiting to happen, I don't find it very difficult to detect.

THE ROAD TO BURNOUT

Let me stress again that I raced down the road to burnout in my own way. Raised and sheltered in the Hutterite-like confines of The Community Farm of the Brethren (founded by my grandfather, the late Julius Kubassek in 1940). I completed my formal education there by the age of fourteen. Within two years of graduating, I was the community's shoe repairman and chickenman. At sixteen, I became interested in electricity and set a goal to become a licensed electrician without serving an apprenticeship. Through a home-study course and some practical experience working in the trade while earning a dollar-a-day, I was licensed by the age of twenty-one. I left the Community Farm on January 01, 1980 with $2,000, determined to make a huge success of myself in the outside business world.

Too inexperienced to know about failure, I went right into business with my oldest brother Dave, forming a plumbing and electrical contracting partnership. Always ambitious, I devoured every book on goal-setting, success, money and business that I could get my hands on. Within six years I had achieved every goal I had set for my entire life; a beautiful wife, an adorable family and the home of my dreams on a hobby farm. I was driving a luxury automobile, owned three businesses and had a net-worth in excess of one million dollars. How did I, how could anyone, move so quickly from success to burnout?

The truth is that many different roads lead to burnout, for business people, executives, working moms, students, administrators and workers. In recent years, I've sent some of my own employees on holidays when they were showing signs of burnout. I've also counseled dozens of others I've come across or have contacted me, - accountants ... consultants ... plumbers ... farmers and pastors.

I sat with one patient for hours during a psychiatric evaluation at the London Psychiatric Hospital. I walked the halls, looking into the blank stares of the patients and wishing I could help each one of them overcome, as I had, the deadly grip of depression.

These people once had been making significant

contributions to society as doctors, dentists, business people, teachers and almost every other profession you can imagine. Now here they sat, incapacitated by that same brilliant mind that had made possible their earlier achievements.

CHAPTER — 2

*O*VER - *COMMITTED? -*
OR OUT OF BALANCE?

BURNOUT, referred to as "the plague of our times" by psychologists, is a term heard with increasing frequency. This is hardly surprising, given that the stress-filled lives we are living at warp speed in the 1990s is causing people from all walks of life to experience burnout as never before.

John Nesbitt says in his book, Megatrends, *"Technology and human potential are the two great challenges and adventures facing humankind today. The great lesson we must learn from the principle of high tech/high touch is a modern version of the ancient Greek ideal — balance....We must learn to balance the material wonders of technology with the spiritual demands of nature."*

At the very heart of our well-being is the need for a healthy integration and balance between the four basic dimensions of life — spiritual, mental, physical and social. There are different ways to help visualize the concept of balance. For me, the old scale of justice helps: the base being our spiritual dimension, the pivot being our mental capacity, one arm being our physical condition and the other being our social lives.

Burnout caused by job stress is a global problem. Read this excerpt from a Japanese newspaper. *"Waitresses in Sweden, postal workers in America, bus drivers in Europe and assembly line workers everywhere are all showing increasing signs of job stress."* - Mainichi Daily News.

A specially-commissioned poll by the Gallop organization shows that 89% of Americans are concerned about "managing their time and energy among the various demands and priorities of life," and that 56% are greatly or very greatly concerned.

According to the same poll, the higher a person's income level is, the more concerned he or she is about balance. Worry over balance peaks among people 30 to 45 years old — people who may be raising a family, climbing the corporate ladder and building a business at the same time.

In a Time/CNN poll of five hundred adults, 69% said they would like to "slow down and live a more relaxed life," compared with only nineteen percent who said they would like to "live a more exciting, faster-paced life." Furthermore, 61% agreed that "earning a living today requires so much effort that it's hard to enjoy life."

One study concluded that the effects of stress are costing about $150 billion a year in the United States. The Canadian Mental Health Association says that depressed workers in Canada cost their employers more than $300 million a year in long-term disability claims. This potentially fatal illness afflicts an estimated 670,000 workers, the association says.

Symptoms of burnout in the workplace include:
- Inability to concentrate and make decisions
- Decreased productivity
- An unusual increase in errors and a decline in dependability
- Irritability and in some cases hostility
- Alcohol or drug abuse
- Negativity

Sources indicate that one out of four workers today is suffering from stress symptoms in one way or another, be it depression, chronic fatigue, chest pains or headaches. It is also believed that, in the very near future, job-related stress will soon be the number one source of worker's compensation claims.

BURNOUT

What is *burnout?* - For me it was a state of spiritual, mental and physical exhaustion that left me without hope, without energy, without any sign of relief. Psychologist Herbert Freudenberger, who may have coined the term, says that *"burnout is a depletion of energy and a feeling of being overwhelmed by other people's problems."* Being in business for myself, I became overwhelmed with my own problems. Molehills became mountains to me. Stepping stones now looked like stumbling blocks.

Psychologist Samuel H. Klarreich, in his book The Stress Solution: A Rational Approach to Increasing Corporate and Personal Effectiveness writes, *"Burnout is the depletion of your resources, both physical and psychological, caused by a compulsive desire to achieve, due to exaggerated expectations which you feel must be fulfilled and which are typically, but not always, job-related. Once these are not fulfilled, there is an overwhelming tendency towards cynicism, pessimism and negativity."*

Is burnout caused by overwork? Ann McGee-Cooper, a brain researcher, says that burnout is *"the result of living out of balance, typically in an all-work/no play spiral."* I am personally convinced that if balance is our number-one priority, it is impossible to burnout from overwork. We all have the same built-in limiting factor called, "The 24-hr. Day."

My own personal experience with burnout brought with it a loss of energy and enthusiasm, of perspective and purpose or in other words, my love of life. Suddenly, it seemed as if all of life's challenges had turned into problems; life didn't seem to be worth living any more. My get-up and go had gotten up and left. The cause of my burnout was living a very imbalanced and stress-filled life. Operating with the unrealistic financial goals I had set for myself, I was left without the social and recreational goals needed to counter-balance the negative mental and physical stress. The business continued to consume more of my waking hours.

My Dad had always told me as a boy *"All work and no play makes Johnny a dull boy,"* (it almost made me a dead boy). I discovered that this rule applies to men as well as boys.

Burnout affected my whole being: physically, mentally and spiritually. Physically I experienced a loss of appetite, insomnia, headaches, chest pains, ulcers, and a constant sense of fatigue. Others also experience high blood pressure, migraines, back pain, strokes and heart attacks.

Mentally, my decisiveness had transformed into confusion; my optimism, into negativism. I became irritable with my family, had difficulty concentrating and found my self-esteem greatly decreased.

Spiritually, I discovered my faith in God had gradually been supplanted by faith in myself. Now that I was feeling down emotionally, I was even losing faith in myself. I felt empty, alone and helpless as I began to recognize my own limitations.

Dr. Hans Selye, to whom we owe much of our contemporary understanding of stress, offers this advice for handling stress that could lead to burnout: *practice self-awareness and be honest with yourself about your personal needs, preferences, abilities and weaknesses; keep an optimistic attitude, putting negative beliefs into perspective and gearing energy to finding positive solutions; make personal choices that are in your best interest; and learn to use your stress-energy, because there is a limited supply.*

BURNOUT CANDIDATES

Type "A" — obsessive-compulsive personalities like me — are the most likely candidates for burnout. Being a workaholic and a success-oriented achiever, I just couldn't say *"No."* I was a driven person, gratified only by accomplishment, caught in the uncontrolled pursuit of expansion. It's the peak performers who have the greatest tendency towards burnout. The low achiever is happy just to rust out!

"In order to suffer from burnout, you must first be on fire," says Elliot Aronson, professor of social psychology at the University of California. Those afire

with high goals and ideals are the most prone to burnout. However, those who suffer burnout are often a company's best people.

SUPER-MOM BURNOUT

The working mom, another likely candidate for burnout, reminds me of a juggler at the circus, who starts with one ball and, before you know it, has half a dozen going at one time. The working mom needs to juggle her husband, her kids, her career, her personal time, her home and the list goes on.

Stay-at-home moms also experience burnout. After a few years of taking care of their children, mothers can become very impatient with them. It feels as if they just keep doing and doing and doing, in a cycle that never ends. The swimming lessons, the piano lessons, ballet, sports, school events, and again the list goes on and on.

MANAGER'S BURNOUT

Managers are also likely candidates for burnout, especially those with the following characteristics:

- High-energy. High-motivation
- A compulsion to do two things at a time (i.e. eat while catching up on their reading)
- A desire to have a significant impact on the organization
- A very serious sense of responsibility
- An openness to new challenges
- A desire to be number one, a success
- An inability to refrain from hurrying the speech of others
- A need to walk, talk and eat rapidly
- Annoyance in watching someone perform a task that they could do faster themselves

HELPER'S BURNOUT

Burnout is also very common in the helping professions, where people work with others in very emotionally demanding situations over a long time.

The nurse caring for a cancer patient, for instance, pours her heart and soul into caring for her patient, only to watch that person slowly fade away. The ER doctor constantly faces intensely emotional emergencies. These people are expected to be professional and personally concerned while being exposed to the physical, psychological, and social problems of their clients.

Teachers do their best to maintain discipline in the classroom, many times without the support of parents. They try to educate, motivate and inspire their students, only to watch some of them drop out and others destroy their lives with drugs. Teachers of the blind, of the deaf, and of those with other physical or mental challenges must deal with the slow learning process and the ever present thought that these children could easily have been their own.

Burnout hits unlikely victims as well. Keith, a capable Christian minister, was full of vigor and creative ideas. He had helped his church to grow from 100 to 300 parishioners in less than three years. Running flat out, Keith's passion for saving souls had become an obsession. It didn't matter to him that he hardly saw his family and his teenage kids were getting into trouble at school, that he didn't follow an exercise program and was grossly overweight, or that he worked seven days a week and hadn't taken a vacation in five years. It didn't matter that is, until one day, Keith collapsed in exhaustion. He shut himself in his bedroom all day long. He felt as if he was in a tunnel with no way out. He had difficulty making decisions, even what to eat for lunch or what clothes to wear. He didn't feel like doing anything. He was completely burned-out.

The "others-centered" orientation that characterizes human service professionals is one cause of burnout. Their sensitivity to the needs of others can be a taxing experience that eventually takes its toll. In response, many learn the hard way the importance of regular physical, mental and emotional withdrawal. They give and give without ever stopping to renew - to refill their tank. They burnout!

STUDENT BURNOUT

The tremendous stress of mental strain, sleep deprivation and unrealistic deadlines all add up to burnout for many students. Medical students especially are put through grueling schedules and assignments supposedly to prepare them for the imbalanced life that follows graduation. In addition, many students without wealthy parents are faced with the financial pressures of earning or borrowing the money needed for tuition.

CHILD BURNOUT

Yes, even children can burnout. The pressures placed on their children by some parents to perform and to become super-kids is causing huge problems. Over-demanding parents sometimes cause teens to run away or even commit suicide. Children are a product of their environment. Without true love and affection in a home, they can experience depression and despair. Many end their life before they have a chance to explore its possibilities.

While some parents place pressure on their children by their demands, parents that are largely absent and/or excessively permissive cause stress as well. Kids need parents that are supportive and available. They are inexperienced at the game of life and learning the rules on their own is very stressful.

Asked to develop a test to screen out those who are likely to burn out, a specialist said that the test should instead be used as a hiring standard. *"What companies need to do," he said, "is to find people that care enough to burn out . . . and then develop programs to combat burnout."* I believe that the best training investment a company can make is to sell its employees on the importance of being balanced. Why have sales training, time management training, and motivational speeches, if employees are too burned out to benefit from them? What they need is life-balance training in order for all other training to make sense and work in harmony.

HOW BURNED OUT ARE YOU?

Ayala Pines and Elliot Aronson, the co-authors of *Career Burnout - Causes And Cures,* have developed a self-diagnostic instrument for calculating your burnout score.

If your score is between 2 and 3, you are doing well. The only suggestion they make is to review your score sheet for honesty. With a score between 3 and 4, it's wise for you to examine your work and life, evaluate your priorities and consider possible changes. With a score higher than 4, you are experiencing burnout and must do something about it. A score higher than 5 is an acute state where there is a need for immediate help.

After you have completed this test, get your spouse to complete it on your behalf to check her opinion of you.

Table 1

How often do you have any of the following experiences?

1	2	3	4	5	6	7
Never	Once in a while	Rarely	Sometimes	Often	Usually	Always

_____ 1. Being tired.

_____ 2. Feeling depressed.

_____ 3. Having a good day.

_____ 4. Being physically exhausted.

_____ 5. Being emotional exhausted.

_____ 6. Being happy.

_____ 7. Being "wiped out."

_____ 8. "Can't take it anymore."

_____ 9. Being unhappy.

_____ 10. Feeling run-down.

_____ 11. Feeling trapped.

_____ 12. Feeling worthless.

_____ 13. Being weary.

_____ 14. Being troubled.

_____ 15. Feeling disillusioned and resentful.

_____ 16. Being weak and susceptible to illness.

_____ 17. Feeling hopeless.

_____ 18. Feeling rejected.

_____ 19. Feeling optimistic.

_____ 20. Feeling energetic.

_____ 21. Feeling anxious.

Computation of score:

Add the values you wrote next to the following items:
1,2,4,5,7,8,9,10,11,12,13,14,15,16,17,18,21 (A) _____.

Add the values you wrote next to the following items:
3,6,19,20 (B) _____, subtract (B) from 32(C) _____.

Add A and C(D) _____.

Divide by 21 _____. This is your burnout score.

BURNOUT PREVENTION

The following list of suggestions can help prevent burnout.

1. Learn to identify the warning signs that indicate burnout is close.

2. Discover the art of setting realistic balanced goals. Learn how in Chapter 10.

3. Learn to manage your stress as an asset, not as a liability.

4   Engage in physical exercise daily - a brisk walk is great.

5. Know how and when to say no.

6. Take control of your thoughts, feelings and behavior.

7. When worry strikes, think of the worst thing that could happen, and say, "So what?"

8. Learn how to relax without feeling guilty. Take a deep breath when you begin to feel anxiety coming on.

9. Adopt an attitude of gratitude. Give thanks daily to your Creator.

10. Respect others and show them your appreciation with praise.

11. Establish your priorities and identify your values.

12. Live your life congruent with your values. Walk your talk.

13. Give twelve hugs every day. Love yourself and others.

14. View failure and obstacles in life as learning experiences, not to be taken too seriously.

15. Avoid negative, destructive thoughts as often as humanly possible. Avoid negative people in the same way.

16. Develop time and life management skills. Don't procrastinate - do it now!

17. Always maintain a sense of humor. If you're not having fun, you're not doing it right!

BROWNOUTS

For several years after burnout, I would occasionally experience what Dr. Robert Schuller calls a *brownout,* meaning *a temporary loss of power.* Being an electrician by trade, I too was very familiar with this term. Many times during an electrical storm or high winds, the electricity goes out and we are in the dark for a while. That's called a blackout. However, sometimes the lights merely flicker and the power is immediately restored. This is called a *brownout.*

These brownouts are our body's alarm system. I discovered, these brownouts were my body's way of warning me that my life was getting out of balance in some area and that I was heading for possible burnout again. These usually meant I was neglecting the spiritual side of my life and had lost touch with God. Don't misunderstand me, being in touch with God won't eliminate your problems, but it sure helps having Him at the controls.

Brownouts were also reminders that I'd been neglecting my physical exercise or that I was accommodating myself to questionable ethics or immoral acts. This temporary overload on my emotional system, would mean that I must immediately rest, evaluate the cause of my stress and take corrective action, asking God for His forgiveness and assistance. It sometimes meant getting up from my desk, closing my office door and pressing the *Do-Not-Disturb* button on my phone. I would then lie flat on the floor and relax my body from the tip of my toes to the top of my head.

RELAX

I still practice relaxation regularly whenever I find myself stressed out and in need of quieting my mind. Although relaxation skills can be performed just about anywhere, they are most effective when practiced in silence and solitude. Get alone in a quiet place if possible. Second, place your body in a position that takes no effort to maintain. You won't want to fall off your chair when your body relaxes.

Next, relaxing a stressed body requires talking to it. At first you may feel strange speaking to your toes as you begin to wiggle them and tell them to relax. As you work your way up your body, speak to each body part and encouraging it to relax. As you finish with one part and move on to the next, do not think about the previous part and imagine that it no longer exists.

After you have worked your way through each external and internal part that you are aware of and come to your brain, think about an icon or object that will help you focus on your Creator. Breath deeply and in rhythm with a positive statement that reminds you of His presence. As mind and body totally relaxes, there comes an awesome sense of peace and tranquillity.

COPING WITH BURNOUT

Burdened with stress from anxieties and the hopelessness of their situations and the hassles of daily life, many people try to drink away their frustrations. They turn to alcohol, the most widely used drug today, to escape the harsh realities of burnout. Others resort to popular prescription drugs to deal with their anxieties. Still others resort to mind-altering drugs such as marijuana and cocaine.

Then there are those who take escapist measures to deal with stress, thereby increasing the frustration. They go on shopping sprees or they put on a masquerade of cheerfulness when, on the inside, they feel totally depressed. Instead of rekindling the dying fire on the inside, most people focus on trying to dilute their stress and anxiety with substances that only speed up the process of burnout. So, what can you do if you feel the fire on the inside going out?

REKINDLING THE FLAME

The steps to rekindling the flame in a burntout life are really no secret at all; they are natural laws or principles that date back to Biblical times.

Step 1. **Stop!** Temporarily change activity and location. The sooner you take step one, the better. You have been heading off course, and the longer you continue, the further you are getting from your destination. As Jim Rohn says, *"You can change direction overnight; it's much more difficult to change destination overnight."*

Step 2. **Look!** Check the fuel gauge. Take a look inside. Ask yourself, *"How have I been living my life over the past six months? Have I been living an incongruent life (Not true to myself and my core values.) ?"*

"How balanced have I been? How much time have I spent with my family or with myself in solitude? Have I been exercising, socializing, playing, praying?"

"How well have I been communicating with my spouse, my family, my co-workers?"

Step 3. **Listen!** Listen to what your body is telling you. Does your engine sound like it needs a tune up? Or maybe an overhaul? Listen to what the people around you are telling you. Right now, your perception may be clouded. When under excessive stress, we tend to make negative estimates of everything and entrap ourselves in pessimistic viewpoints. Most times there is no basis for such uncharacteristic, negative thinking.

Step 4. **Take Control!** Easier said, then done! However, changing direction always requires being in control. And right now, you don't like the direction you're headed in. In order to overcome the feeling of helplessness, you must take control of your thoughts and behavior. We may not have control of which thoughts come into our minds, but we do have control over which thoughts we allow to remain there. Just by initiating positive thoughts and actions, we can crowd out any negative thoughts.

Step 5. **Change Direction!** We have all heard the classic definition of insanity: *"Doing the same thing, but somehow expecting different results."* If you don't like the looks of the destination you are heading towards, it's time to change it, especially if the destination is burnout. Take action to change immediately! Don't procrastinate.

Step 6. **Stay on Course!** Don't drift. Keep checking the road map. The only way to stay on course is to keep checking the road map. Without a road map, such as this book, you may tend to drift off course. Regularly review your values, your dreams and your goals. Keep your eyes focused on your intended destination.

Step 7. **Don't Travel Alone!** Build yourself a support system of family and friends. We all need someone in whom we can confide our personal feelings.

Feel free to use the resources of our religious centers and mental health services. Your pastor can provide invaluable spiritual support if you let him.

While we all need human support, each one of us also needs an intimate relationship with our Creator if our life is to have meaning. Without an attachment to something larger than ourselves, we all have difficulty in coping with feelings of helplessness.

Step 8. **Keep Your Windshield Clean!** Don't let the bugs accumulate on your windshield, they'll distract you and cloud your vision. Those bugs are your negative thoughts, your negative relatives, and the negative media. As Jeffrey Gitomer, the author of The Sales Bible says, *"People rain on your parade because they don't have a parade of their own."*

Keep your vision clear by the power of association. Surround yourself with like-minded, positive people that appreciate and encourage you. They pour gas on your fire; you feel better just being in their presence.

Please, not the wipers!

CHAPTER — 3

RAISING THE BAR TOO HIGH

"A person without a goal is like a ship without a rudder, but a person with unrealistic goals is one headed for trouble."

Another cause of my burnout was the fact that my goals were set unrealistically. I had set my goals high, aware that they had to make me stretch but unaware that we are all like elastic bands: if we stretch too far we eventually snap. When a goal appeared to be within reach, I would immediately revise my goal upward out of reach again, always within an unrealistic time frame. The horrendous amount of self-induced stress I was under took its toll on me mentally and physically.

At the age of twenty-one, I set a goal of having a net worth of 1 million dollars by the time I was 50. I went right into business with the determination of a bulldog to achieve it. For starters, I would never work for anyone but myself.

My brother Dave said to me just before leaving the farm, "Ben, you can do anything you want to do, if you want to do it badly enough." I believed him. I wanted to be a financial success more than anything in the world.

FARM BOY MAKES IT BIG

Within eighteen months of leaving home, I was not only married to the girl of my dreams, but also operating a successful plumbing and electrical business with my brother Dave. We were in the midst of the 1981/82 recession. Here I was, just new in business, the country in a deep recession, and I decided to buy land to build a home for my wife and me. This wasn't just any lot. It was 50 acres of land with the Nith River running through it just 3 miles from the Community Farm where I was born and raised. The price tag was $96,000 dollars. After all, I did have $2,000 dollars in the bank. The vendor was willing to hold a mortgage for the entire purchase price, I was convinced that I was going to be a success in business and, to boot, I had nothing to lose.

You can just imagine the looks I got from bankers when I went to them looking for a mortgage to build the house of my dreams on a piece of land I had already mortgaged to the hilt. Without a track record as a borrower, without experience as a businessman and without any collateral, I was deemed a bad risk. They tried to explain to me how my Gross Debt Servicing Ratio was way out of whack and that nobody could make $1,200 monthly mortgage payments plus taxes and utilities on an income of $2,000/month.

Every bank I visited turned me down. However, they all offered to finance me after I had proved myself in business and had acquired some assets that I could give them as collateral. When leaving their offices, I would say "It sounds like you're prepared to loan me money when I can prove beyond all reasonable doubt that I have no need for it."

NO MONEY - NO PROBLEM

Not finding the money was not going to stop me from building a house. I just went ahead and started the foundation of our new home in December 1981, less than two years after I left the farm. People thought I was crazy. My dad even tried to convince my lawyer at the time to talk me out of purchasing the land. This was a recession; however, trades-people were looking for work, prices were down and I wanted a house of my own. In sixty days, my wife and I moved into our new home without a mortgage. However, I did have some outstanding accounts with my subtrades and suppliers.

Returning to my local bank, I informed the manager that I had just built the house he had refused to finance and asked him to reconsider giving me the mortgage. He agreed. I hadn't even begun to start worrying whether I would be able to pay all the bills I had incurred building our home. The home that I had envisioned as a farm boy earning a dollar a day, just two years before, was now precisely the way I had seen it in my mind's eye. Today, we still live in that beautiful home in a peaceful country setting just a five minute drive from my office.

By the time I reached twenty-seven years of age, I had achieved a net worth of over one million dollars. I had also already re-set my financial goals to earn a million dollars a year, a goal that I well exceeded by the time I was thirty years old. Having achieved the million dollars a year of personal income, I still did not feel as if I had reached my full earning potential. It was then that I set a goal to give away a million dollars in one year. Selfish goal setting and goal achievement were both losing their appeal.

You may think "WOW" what super-success in reaching goals. In reality, I never did feel a sense of victory because, whenever I was getting within view of a goal, I would re-set it to a level that was out of sight. To me a goal within reach was no goal at all. So I set unrealistic goals for every area of my life that was important to me at the time. Unfortunately, the only area of my life important to me at that time was the financial area.

EXCITING – YET REALISTIC

The key to preventing yourself from setting unrealistic goals is to maintain a balance between what is realistic and what presents us with an exciting challenge.

The real reason for my unrealistic goal setting was the fact I was a perfectionist. I didn't just strive for excellence; I was striving for perfection. What is the difference? Fritz Ridenour says it best in his book *The Traveler's Guide To Life At Warp Speed.*

> Perfectionism sets impossible goals. Excellence sets high standards within reach.
> Perfectionism values "what I do," excellence values "who I am."
> Perfectionism dwells on mistakes and excellence learns from them.
> Perfectionism says "I've got to be number one," and excellence says "I did my best and I am satisfied."

An athlete needs to progressively set higher and higher goals but always begins with a realistic goal. Unrealistic goals not only create undue stress but also make us feel discouraged by our failure to reach our goals, goals that were set too high in the first place.

Remember the advice of Jonathan Kozol - *"Pick battles big enough to matter, small enough to win."*

Failing to identify the resources, the time and the effort required to reach our goals will often result in us setting goals that are just simply unrealistic. In most cases those who raise the bar too high fall flat on their face.

When you aim for perfection you discover a moving target.

– George Fisher

CHAPTER — 4

*B*URNING THE CANDLE
AT BOTH ENDS

THE LAST THING I wanted to hear when I was going through burnout was "that I was a workaholic." First of all, being referred to as such would have implied that I was not in control of an area of my life, that I had an addiction. Not me! I was always in control of everything. Or so I thought.

I began thinking to myself, what is a workaholic? According to Wayne Oates, who coined the term, it connotes an addiction to work. Typically, workaholics are people for whom work has become a single, all-involving preoccupation. It is the only thing in life that seems to matter to them, the only thing that makes them feel alive. They invest all their time and energy in it, so there is little or nothing left for other people or activities. That sounded too much like me!

"The workaholic enjoys nothing except an occasional good meal, constant supplies of work, and a good bed to fall into from sheer exhaustion. This goes on until death" —Wayne Oates — *Confessions Of A Workaholic*

Just as devoutly religious people get their sense of "significance" from their religion, workaholics get it from their work. Since they don't need much besides work to meet their needs, most limit themselves to relationships that don't interfere with their work. Some workaholics choose to remain single for that very reason. Some find a workaholic spouse that won't interfere with their schedule. Others simply marry workaholics with the idea that somehow they change the person they are marrying into the person they want to live with.

In the most common situation, one spouse is a workaholic and the other is quite the opposite. Speaking from experience, I can tell you that this situation makes for a very stressful marriage. As a reformed workaholic, I can assure you that the more we experience stress in our homes as a result of our workaholism, the more we seek opportunity to escape. We go to work early, we stay late and we bring work home.

DOUBLE TROUBLE

When both mates are workaholics, their involvement with each other is, of course, very limited. In this case, the children are neglected and suffer. Many people can identify with growing up with a workaholic parent, but as a child I knew what it was like to have two parents who were both very hard workers. They absolutely loved their work. For the first twelve years of my life, I did not know what a family vacation was, nor had I ever seen my parents even take as much as a day off to get away and spend time exclusively with each other - in order to rest from their work and invest in their relationship.

The most traumatic experience for workaholics is burnout caused by the very thing they love - work. Since relationships have not been a high priority, to whom does the workaholic turn to for support? In my experience as a workaholic going through burnout, I looked around me for support and found myself pretty much alone.

THE ADDICTION

The idea of a drug addict or alcoholic we can understand, but we seldom give much thought to the workaholic. Possibly one of the most destructive of all addictions is the compulsion to work. Add to that the fact that it often goes untreated because it is the only addiction that makes you look like a hero. Workaholism has destroyed families, marriages and health, leading people down the path we call burnout, some till they reach the precipice known as suicide.

The balanced person can work with joy and deep satisfaction, but for the workaholic, the job or business becomes his god and the place of employment is the temple where he worships.

THE SYMPTOMS OF WORKAHOLISM

1. Workaholics work long hours. It is not uncommon for a workaholic to maintain a 14 hour/ day pace for six days a week. They also love to talk about how early they got to work, how late they stayed and how little sleep they got the night before. Before my burnout, a seventy-five hour work week was normal for me. I have since discovered that there is little relation

between productivity and the hours worked and that I now accomplish more in fifty-five hours than I once did in seventy-five.

2. Workaholics find it very difficult to say "NO" to people making demands on their time, often taking on more and more to please others and to be accepted. They also have trouble delegating responsibility since they feel they are the only ones who can do it right. They have trouble accepting the fact that they do have limits.

3. Workaholics talk about work. People talk about the subjects that interest them; for the workaholic, that's work. They seldom talk about or enjoy a hobby and rarely mention their family in conversation.

4. Workaholics feel guilty when they relax. The family vacation is a waste of time for a workaholic, and an afternoon of golf causes more guilt than it's worth. An evening out with their spouse is easily pre-empted by something of higher priority at the office.

5. Workaholics' habits are destructive to their health. Physical ailments such as heart disease and circulatory problems are common among workaholics. Our bodies were not created to be used as machines.

According to the Harris Poll, by 1987 the average work week had risen to 46.6 hours from 40.6 hours in 1973. During that same period, leisure time shrank from 26.2 hours a week down to 16.2 hours a week.

THE CAUSES OF WORKAHOLISM:

1. Greed — For the self-centered person, greed can be a major cause of this addiction.

2. Adrenaline high — In many cases, the person has become addicted to adrenaline, (the legal way to get a high).

3. Imbalanced goals — When our goals all revolve around our career and our finances, we tend to allow our work to consume us.

So, how do you develop a high performance attitude without becoming a workaholic? The key is *Balance*. Have a passion for your family, friends, and hobbies as well as your work. Build your relationships with the same zeal you build your business or career. With balance, you get more done at work, and you have more fun with your family and your friends than you ever thought possible. You'll discover that the only difference between work and play is your attitude.

Can a person work up to 65 hours a week and still be balanced? I believe so. Here's how I do it:

Total Hours Available to Everyone In a Week	**168**
Personal Time (Reading, Thinking & Planning)	10
Family Time (Playing, Walking, Swimming)	14
Eating	14
Working	65
Sleeping (6 hours/night)	42
Grooming (Showering, Shaving, Dressing)	3
Exercising	3
Driving Time	7
Church Attendance	3
TV	7

CHAPTER — 5

STRESSED OUT

STRESS:

The word "stress" comes from the Latin word strictus, which means to be drawn tight. When we are as tight as rubber bands, we show the tension in headaches, tight muscles, digestive problems and insomnia. Stress is what occurs when the demands of the situation, in the person's eyes, clearly exceed the resources of the person to handle them.

AS OUR WORLD ACCELERATES...

Stress has always been around. As life accelerates, so does the level of stress each one of us is under. Everybody's feeling its effect. There are no antibiotics that can touch it. Scientists can't even spot it with a microscope.

Everyone agrees that these are high pressure times, and many people are complaining of being worn out, overworked, used up, and burned out. The uncertainty of a secure job and the constant change in organizations are just wearing many employees down.

The rate of change, and the stress associated with it, will not slow down in the future but will accelerate. Our only hope is to learn how to handle stress better.

Dr. Hart, in his book *Adrenaline & Stress,* states that the essence of stress is over-arousal and the addiction to adrenaline. He also states that 50 to 70 percent of patients going to general physicians are there primarily because of stress-related problems.

Try To Control Only The Controllable

Events themselves are not stressful. It's how we perceive them that makes us feel tense. In general, stress comes from feeling out of control. The key to relieving stress is to change the things we have the power to change and accept those we don't. Always ask yourself if you are in a position to control the situation or will you just get emotionally drained trying?

Trying to control matters out of your control is a bad investment of energy and a pure waste of time. As Yogi Berra said *"If the people don't want to come out to the park, nobody is going to stop them."*

Low-Stress Work Settings

The end result of personal and job-related stress without balance is: Burnout. The most stressful occupations, according to psychologists, are those dealing with other people's problems (i.e., pastors, medical people, social workers, etc.). It's true that some occupations are less stressful than others; however, today there is no such thing as a low-stress organization that's on track to survive.

Failing to change can bring relief from stress in the short-term. We can buy a little time - but to do so we have to mortgage our future.

The Two Kinds Of Stress

Dr. Hans Selye, defines stress as our body's response to any demand made upon it. He divides stress into two kinds: (1) *distress* — excessive levels of continued, damaging stress and (2) *eustress* — a good, positive kind of stress one feels at times of happiness, fulfillment, or satisfaction.

Although some stress is necessary for learning and growth in everyday life, chronic and huge amounts of stress can debilitate people physically, mentally and spiritually. We all need some stress or tension to keep us in tune, much like the strings on a guitar. With just the right tension on each string, we have harmony. But just overtighten one of those babies and see what happens. It snaps! Therefore, what we need to know is, not how to eliminate the stress or tension from our lives, but how to keep it balanced and within our limits.

Maintaining a stress balance in our lives is similar to maintaining the balance in a bank account. When our balance is running low due to the withdrawals caused by negative stress, we need to make deposits. Deposits of positive stress are required to keep ourselves from stress-induced bankruptcy or burnout.

Stress, in itself, will not lead one to burnout. However, living a stressful life without a balance between the spiritual, mental, physical and social, is a dangerous road to travel that can imperceptibly lead to the brink of a precipice, the precipice of burnout, depression and, in some cases, suicide.

THE CAUSES OF STRESS

Job-related - The most common causes of stress today are job-related. As we look at burnout victims, we see that all jobs create some stress. However, in each job, the key to handling the stress is to gain some sort of control. The feeling of loss of control can be one of the early warning signs of burnout. Key contributing factors to stress in our vocations are as follows:

(a) *Inexperience* - The young executive promoted to a new position in management will experience a great deal more stress than a veteran who has spent twenty years doing the same job. Education and aptitude are no substitute for experience. This probably explains why the most dynamic and promising young employees are the most common victims of stress and burnout. They are promoted and given responsibilities beyond that which their experience has equipped them for.

(b) *Deadlines* - As our pace in life quickens, so do the number of deadlines we face. The meaning of the word deadline is clear: *"if you're not across the line at a given time, you're dead."* Deadlines create pressure, and pressure creates stress. Goals with deadlines create pressure, that's why most people choose to dream rather than set goals.

(c) *Risk* - Every time we take a risk, there is stress created in our bodies. Perhaps it would be fair to say that the stress results from the anxiety of not knowing the outcome of the decisions that we make. This is where our faith in God is helpful since He knows the end from the beginning. When we take our faith and place it entirely in ourselves, we are subjecting our bodies and minds to unnecessary stress.

(d) **Wrong Job** - The stress we are experiencing may be a sign we are in the wrong job and need a change of career direction. I've always told my employees *"There is only one thing better than doing what you like, that's liking what you do. So if you don't like your job, quit!"*

(e) **Change** - Organizational change is going to happen whether or not you like it. Instead of fighting change, invest your energy in making quick adjustments. Being a helicopter pilot, I can tell you that the more quickly you adjust the controls to compensate for any changes in wind direction, velocity or turbulence, the less compensation is required. The longer you wait to adjust the controls, the more drastic your movements are. Life is much like flying a helicopter: to enjoy a smooth flight, we need to feel the changes happening before they are visible and then to subtly adjust the controls.

Fear and worry — These two are probably the most common causes of stress. I have never seen anyone suffering from stress who wasn't worried or fearful about something. More on this in Chapter 8.

COMMON SYMPTOMS OF DISTRESS

Here are some of the more commonly accepted symptoms of distress:

- Skin diseases
- Frequent headaches
- Tiredness on waking
- Insomnia
- Memory loss
- Irritability / short temper
- Loss of sense of humor
- Lack of ambition

- The desire to avoid people
- Intestinal disorders (i.e. indigestion, constipation
- Nervous trembling of the hands.

J.C. PENNY

Millions of people have visited a J. C. Penny store, one of the world's largest chains of department stores, however, very few people know of one of the most important events of J. C. Penny's life.

Having survived the economic crash of 1929, J. C. Penny's business was still intact, but he had made some unwise personal commitments. The commitments worried him so much he couldn't sleep. The stress from this chronic fatigue depressed his immune system. He then suffered a relapse of the chicken-pox virus that had been silently hiding in the nerves ever since he had the rash as a child. The recurrence of this virus is called *shingles,* a disease that causes great annoyance and severe pain. He was hospitalized, but the sedatives he was given brought him no relief and he spent the night tossing around on his bed. A series of events had broken him so mentally and physically that he was overwhelmed with the fear of death. He wrote farewell letters to his wife and son, since he didn't expect to live until morning.

That morning Mr. Penny awoke to the sound of singing in the chapel. He managed to pull himself together, walked down to the chapel and as he entered, the group was singing *God Will Take Care Of You.* Following a scripture reading and prayer, suddenly, as J. C. Penny writes *"something happened. I can't explain it. I can only call it a miracle. I felt as if I had been instantly lifted out of the darkness of a dungeon into warm, brilliant sunlight. It felt as if I had been transported from hell to paradise. I knew that God in His love was there to help me. From that day to this, my life has been free from worry. I am seventy-one years old and the most dramatic and glorious minutes of my life were those I spent in that chapel that morning: "God Will Take Care of You."*

STRESS MEASUREMENT

Many times in our lives, situations and experiences cause varying amounts of stress, even though sometimes we are not consciously aware of it. The following is a list of common stressors you may have experienced in the last twelve months:

EVENT	Value	Score
Your spouse or significant other died	10	
You got divorced	8	
A close family member died	7	
Experienced marital relationship problems	6	
Started a new business venture	6	
Broke the law and got caught	6	
Experienced personal illness or injury	5	
Got fired from your job	5	
Got pregnant	4	
A new baby arrived	4	
Experienced financial difficulties	4	
Started a new job	3	
Experienced a change in lifestyle	3	
Moved residence	2	
Had mortgage payments to make	2	
Took a vacation	1	
Broke the law without getting caught	1	
Misc.		
Enter your total stress rating here	_____	

Now assign values to your particular stresses by comparing them to those on the scale. The ratings apply only to stresses you have undergone in the last 12 months. If your total is over 30, look out! You have an above 75% chance of a serious change in health within the next year. If your total is less than 15 units, you have a 25% chance of a serious change in health in the next year. Up to 30 gives you a 50% chance.

Chains always break at the weakest links. For some people, that serious change in health could be ulcers; for others, it may be heart attacks or even cancer.

Looking at statistics, it appears that 20% of people in the high stress group will not have any change in health. It seems these people are immune to stress. Obviously, they have achieved a balance to their lives that the 80% have not.

Peter G. Hanson, M. D. in his book *The Joy of Stress* has devised — *The Hanson Scale Of Stress Resistance* — to measure your choices in response to stress and show the areas needing improvement. I recommend that you read his book. It's easy to read and contains a wealth of information on the subject of stress.

A THREE-STEP RECIPE

One day while chatting with a group of medical colleagues, Dr. Hans Selye agreed to sum up thirty years of work on stress research by giving them his three-step secret recipe for dealing with life.

First: Decide if you are a "race horse" or a "turtle."

Race horses are the *Type A* people who race through life, stimulated by working fast, hard and long. Without the passing lane and goal lists, their day is a boring waste of time.

Turtles - *Type B* folks on the other hand, are at the other end of the spectrum. You stop by their desk in the morning and their date-books and to-do lists are blank. They take life just one minute at a time.

Second: Choose your own goals in life. Too often our goals are someone else's ideas of what we should do with our lives.

Third: Adopt the strategy that Selye described as *altruist egotism* — "looking out for oneself by being necessary to others and earning their good will."

LACK OF PHYSICAL EXERCISE

Regular physical exercise according to the medical profession, creates endorphins that act as natural tranquilizers in our bodies and help us handle stress.

In my own experience it was shortly after I sat down behind a desk and was no longer physically working with the tools as an electrician that I experienced *Burnout*. I went from being very active to being almost totally physically inactive without realizing it or, shall I say, without really understanding how the lack of physical exercise would affect my ability to handle stress. However, ignorance is no excuse for disobeying any law, including the law of *Balance*. The negative effects are guaranteed whether we understand and accept them or not. Dr. George Sheehan says *"Man was not meant to be at rest. If fitness goes, can the mind be far behind?"*

During my experience with burnout, I often found it impossible to release the negative thoughts from my mind, so sleep was often impossible. Fortunately, prescribed sedation helped me get the healing sleep I required and did not leave me with any addiction to sedatives.

21 STEPS TO A LESS STRESSFUL LIFE

1. Learn some relaxation techniques.

2. Take a hot bath.

3. Get a massage.

4. Exercise three to five times per week for twenty to thirty minutes. Work yourself into a sweat. Fitness reduces stress.

5. Don't sweat about the small stuff. Keep things in perspective. Balance in life is the key.

6. Drink plenty of water and less caffeine. This helps cleanse your body and improves your health.

7. Eat right. Eliminate fats from your diet. Eat lots of fruits and vegetables.

8. Be thankful. Count your blessings every day.

9. Forgive others. Grudges are too heavy to be carried around.

10. Take time for solitude. Meditate.

11. Learn to laugh. Lighten up. Humor heals.

12. When you begin to worry about a situation, think of the worst thing that could happen and say, "so what?"

13. Get to bed earlier if you're not getting enough sleep. Most people sleep a half hour too long every morning. Arise early.

14. Think positive and be optimistic. Expect the best.

15. Recharge your batteries. Have fun. Get yourself a hobby. Write this as "me time" on your calendar.

16. Set realistic personal goals that make you reach.

17. Be sure you are following the right road map.

18. Develop better time management habits. Focus on one thing at a time.

19. Learn to say "NO" with a smile. Don't commit to too many things.

20. Spend lots of quality time with those you love. After you're dead, they won't care how much time you spent at the office.

21. Simplify your life.

The secret is not to try to avoid stress, but to try to balance your life so that the good stress outweighs the bad.

HOW WELL ARE YOU COPING WITH STRESS?

Here are some positive lifestyle behaviors and thoughts to help you deal with stress. How well are you doing?

How often do you...	Never	Hardly Ever	Some-times	Often
1. Have optimistic thoughts about life.	0	1	2	3
2. Spend time with valued friends.	0	1	2	3
3. Exercise aerobically 3 times/week.	0	1	2	3
4. Assert your needs at work and at home.	0	1	2	3
5. Relate well to your spouse.	0	1	2	3
6. Eat breakfast.	0	1	2	3
7. Take private, peaceful time for yourself.	0	1	2	3
8. Maintain your proper weight.	0	1	2	3
9. Speak openly about your feelings.	0	1	2	3
10. Eat a balanced diet.	0	1	2	3
11. Consult health professionals as required.	0	1	2	3
12. Enjoy affection and intimacy.	0	1	2	3
13. Organize your time efficiently.	0	1	2	3
14. Get 7-8 hours of sleep at least 4 nights a week	0	1	2	3
15. Look forward to work.	0	1	2	3

How often do you...

	Never	Hardly Ever	Some-times	Often
16. Accomplish a task you planned.	0	1	2	3
17. Participate in sports, recreation, and hobbies.	0	1	2	3
18. Keep your finances in order.	0	1	2	3
19. Define and achieve goals	0	1	2	3
20. Get strength from your spiritual beliefs.	0	1	2	3
21. Play and have fun.	0	1	2	3
22. Feel good about your accomplishments.	0	1	2	3
23. Discuss concerns with a supportive person.	0	1	2	3
24. Practice relaxation techniques 10-15 minutes daily.	0	1	2	3
25. Believe you control most of your life.	0	1	2	3

Add up your score. TOTAL:_____ A score of 65 or higher shows you are managing stress very well. Between 50 and 64 means you can improve. Below 50 is poor. Take a look at all the 0's and 1's you scored. Come up with strategies for increasing these helpful behaviors. Then take a look at all the 2's and 3's and commit yourself to keeping up the good work. Your body will thank you.

Mr. Smith, your banker's on line one.

CHAPTER — 6

NEGLECT THE BODY AND YOUR MIND WILL FOLLOW

YOU CAN'T LIVE a balanced life without living on a balanced diet. So much has been written on this subject, yet daily I witness people eating themselves to an early grave. Perhaps it is only a matter of self discipline, but a book on balanced living would not be complete without a chapter on nutrition.

What Is Health?

What makes a healthy person? To rephrase the question, what makes a person healthy? Is health the absence of illness? Can one be healthy without being physically fit? Does physical fitness translate into good health? Let's explore the answers together.

Health, defined simply as a state or condition, is relative. But relative to what? Perhaps we need a standard or benchmark based on the science of medicine and the philosophy of naturopathy.

NUTRITION

I believe our common sense is the diet plan each one of us was given at birth. If only we would follow it with some self control, most of us would be better off.

Here are a few tips:

1. Stop drinking sugar in your coffee and tea, and in thirty days you will never miss it.
2. Avoid adding salt to your foods.
3. Quit eating as soon as you feel satisfied.

Before burnout, my eating habits were awful. I would grab a burger and some fries or a sandwich and eat on the run between service calls. I would seldom stop for a decent lunch. Now I relax for an hour while I am eating a balanced meal. I have found that eating can actually be enjoyable.

Zig Ziglar asks this question in his seminars, *"If you had a million dollar race horse, would you keep him up all night drinking coffee and alcohol and smoking cigarettes and expect him to race the next day? What about a ten dollar dog or a five dollar cat? Well, then, why do you do that to your billion dollar body?"*

Coffee, soda pop and alcohol are probably the three most common drinks in our society and none of the three are particularly healthy. Limiting my caffeine intake to three cups of coffee a day has greatly reduced the amount of anxiety I experience while under stress. Since coffee stimulates our body to produce adrenaline, we become as addicted to adrenaline as we are to caffeine.

What we drink is as important as what we eat. Dr. Peter G. Hanson says in his book, *The Joy of Stress, "I recommend (and drink) eight glasses of water a day. This is particularly important for anyone experiencing a lot of stress."*

EXERCISE

Exercise not an option. Inactivity kills! It stagnates the brain and poisons the body. This is not some philosophical concept. It is science and medical fact. The fittest generally live the longest and are the healthiest.

Regular and moderate exercise offers many benefits: a feeling of well-being, increased self-confidence, and reduced irritability and fatigue. Above all, research studies show that a person who exercises becomes noticeably healthier.

The more physically active a person is, the lower the risk of suffering a heart attack. Losing an uncle at 38 to a killer heart attack was enough to convince me! Exercise can also help relieve anxiety and tension found in high-pressure work or in challenging life circumstances.

For weight control, exercise offers a double benefit: it not only uses up calories directly, but extra calories continue to be burned up by the body up to 15 hours after the exercise. In general, exercise decreases appetite, helping the body to readjust food intake to energy expenditure.

With all the benefits of exercise, why are more people not doing it? I'll tell you why. Because it's easy to do and it's even easier not to do!

Dr. Kenneth Cooper says that when you exercise, you activate the pituitary gland, flooding the system with endorphins, which are two hundred times more powerful than morphine. As a result, for the next one to three hours, your energy level is higher and your creativity is at its peak.

The Benefits Of Exercising Are Many

1. It helps reduce tension, anxiety, depression and other symptoms of stress.

2. It improves our ability to think and concentrate.

3. It increases our energy level, making us feel great.

4. It improves our endurance and the length of our life.

5. It strengthens our cardiovascular system.

6. It uplifts us mentally, helping us feel positive.

The key is to play hard physically if you want to work hard mentally yet not burn out. The harder I work with my mind, the more time I spend exercising.

Your exercise time can also be your time of solitude. However, if you have trouble with self-discipline, exercising with a buddy can provide the accountability you need. My jogging buddy is my oldest son, Daniel. He is only 11, but he keeps me going when I feel like stopping.

SLEEP

Adequate, efficient, restful sleep is as important as exercise in combating stress, but it is absolutely essential for recovery from a burnout experience. The sub-conscious mind continues to work while we are asleep. I realized that working in the office till late at night or watching the eleven o'clock news were both poor ways to prepare myself for a refreshing sleep. Instead, you might wish to read a good book or relax in a tub of hot water just before crawling into bed. Perhaps you may even be fortunate enough to have your mate give you a massage before falling off into a peaceful sleep.

TOBACCO

"Tobacco kills three times more Canadians than alcohol, AIDS, illicit drugs, suicide and murder all combined. Thirty years after science established cigarettes as a major cause of disease, the number of people dying from tobacco products continues to rise. That's more than forty thousand Canadians a year."

– January 21, 1995 The Financial Post

I don't need to say anymore than that. If you smoke, quit!

THE MAGIC OF MASSAGE

In today's fast-paced world, there is a simple solution to counter the stress of high-tech. It's called "high-touch" or "massage." In a society of "instant everything" we all seem to be running flat out. Our bodies get sick to slow us down, and we wonder what happened.

One of the oldest healing therapies for "Hurry Sickness," and for many other illnesses, is the healing touch of Massage Therapy. And yet, what amazes me is how misunderstood and unknown this therapy is.

Every living creature has a craving and a need to be touched. Touch is one of our basic human needs - as important as food and water. Massage Therapy acts as the perfect antidote for stress, while fulfilling our need for touch. Massage sends a message to the body to slow down and relax. With this relaxation comes a harmony, a sense of wholeness and inner peace.

My massage therapist, Mrs. Wilma Bolton, has to be the most loving and caring person on earth. She is absolutely wonderful. Let me share with you what it's like to be pampered by her for one hour.

As the healing, soothing massage begins, Mrs. Bolton, checks with you to be certain that you are comfortable, *"Would like the window open so that you can hear the sound of the water falling over the dam outside, or would you prefer the window closed?" - "Would you like the music a little softer perhaps?" - "How is the room temperature?" - "Are you comfortable?".*

When she is certain that everything is just perfect, she begins, in quiet tone, to coach you to relax. *"Now take all your worries, your cares, the things that you have to do, and drop them into a basket outside the door. You can pick them up on your way out. This is your time to relax your mind and your body. It is your time to heal."* Then for an hour she works those tense muscles, muscles you didn't even know you had.

At the end of the end of each session, I feel as if all the stresses and worries in life have been erased and I get to start over from point zero. After a massage session, I feel as if my creativity and my problem-solving ability have been boosted. I feel terrific!

Self-Test - Do I Need A Massage

This is a simple test to determine if massage would be beneficial for you. Think about the past year and rate yourself using the following scale.

0 = Not true for me

5 = Slightly true for me

6 = Generally true for me

7 = Very true for me

____ 1. I get sick two or three times a year.

____ 2. I feel pressured.

____ 3. I get headaches.

____ 4. I sometimes wake up tired or exhausted.

____ 5. I seem to forget things more easily nowadays.

____ 6. I have trouble falling asleep.

____ 7. I have gastro-intestinal problems.

____ 8. I have high blood-pressure.

____ 9. I have aches and pains.

____ 10. I feel alone and unconnected.

____ 11. I have anxiety attacks.

____ 12. I sometimes feel tired and worn out.

____ 13. I'm less enthusiastic about life lately.

____ 14. I worry more than I used to.

____ 15. My neck and shoulders feel tight.

____ 16. I feel burnt out by day's end.

____ 17. My sex drive has changed (not for the better).

____ 18. I have more trouble focusing.

____ 19. My mind is not as clear as it used to be.

____ 20. I don't seem to have enough time for what I want to do.

____ TOTAL SCORE

What your score means:

1 - 20   **Excellent.** You are really taking care of yourself.

21-50   **Normal.** A massage session would be therapeutic and fun.

51-75   **Caution area.** Time to take some action and get your life in control. Slow down a little and get a massage.

76-99   **Burn-out area.** You may be about to have some serious health problems. Time to re-evaluate your life and get a massage now.

100+   **Danger zone.** Did you really score over 100? It is time to make some major changes in your life. Get a massage today!

THE WONDER OF CHIROPRACTIC

Chiropractic has been an important part of my life since I was 14 years old. Fortunately, my father has always been a big believer in this discipline. It was he who introduced me to its wonders.

In school I was always the weakling, the one who was pushed around by the other kids because I was skinny and weak, and didn't fight back. I still remember being punched in the stomach by one of the bullies in our school one day. My oldest brother was looking on and I thought he would come to my rescue. But as I looked up from my kneeling position, I realized that I wasn't going to get any help. I was on my own. I decided then and there, that what I lacked physically, I would make up for intellectually. However, the next kid that pushed me down, threw my back out of commission.

For five years, I endured the pain of a sore back. I visited a chiropractor up to three times a week during those years. His adjustments made the pain bearable.

I can state from experience that chiropractic is truly *health care*, not *disease care*. The primary role of the chiropractor is to locate, correct, and prevent spinal subluxations (a mis-aligned vertebra causing nerve impingement), so that every tissue and organ of the body is well connected and receives proper neurological control from the brain.

If something as safe, effective, and cost-efficient as a chiropractic treatment can improve my health, I'm in. Our bodies deserve the best care we can give them.

I also like any cure that focuses on the cause, not the symptoms. That's what this whole book is about! I just realized, that's probably why chiropractors don't prescribe drugs. What a concept! Fix the cause and you'll not have to worry about the symptoms.

Chiropractors promote a natural approach to achieving and maintaining good health. They believe that drugs or surgery should be used only after all other options have been exhausted or when a patient's life is threatened. The efforts of chiropractors throughout the years, have helped millions achieve a better level of health. No wonder it has expanded to become the second largest health care profession in the world.

CHAPTER — 7

*E*MOTIONAL OVERLOAD

EMOTION IS A *"stirred up reaction such as love, hate, fear, anger or grief."* According to psychologists, an emotion is aroused when a person views something as either good or bad. However, an emotion does not always have an external cause; it can also be created internally, that is, by a person's thoughts. We are the source of all our emotions. Therefore, feeling good is a decision!

We all have emotions, and those of us who do not hide our emotions are referred to as *emotional.* Many psychologists believe that we are born without emotions and that we learn our emotions the same way we learn to read and write. Our parents even teach us how to react emotionally to certain circumstances.

TWO KINDS OF EMOTIONS

Psychologists say there are two types of emotions: negative emotions and positive emotions. Negative emotions, including anger, fear and despair, make us feel unhappy or dissatisfied. Positive emotions, including love, joy and hope, are aroused by something that appeals to us.

Emotions come in varying degrees of strength. For example, we could call a very happy person *overjoyed.* Unfortunately, happiness is only possible if we learn to cope with our negative emotions.

Emotions can help us. Some emotions cause our nervous system to send signals to various glands and organs, telling them that we need to defend ourselves. For example, in fear, the adrenal gland empties a hormone called adrenaline into the bloodstream, increasing the heartrate and raising the blood pressure. Much blood shifts from our digestive organs to the brain and skeletal muscles. The breathing rate increases as large amounts of sugar are dumped into the bloodstream. These emergency measures give the body added energy to face the crisis at hand.

While the hormone *adrenaline* causes the face to go pale and the mouth to go dry when we experience fear, the hormone called noradrenalin, causes our face to become flushed when we are angry.

EMOTIONAL OVERLOAD

If changes in our body continue for a prolonged period of time, tissue damage can result. For example, constant worry and fear can produce stomach ulcers. Strong emotions can make it hard to think, concentrate and solve problems. Worry will drain valuable mental energy needed to function creatively.

Emotional overload occurs when pent-up emotions becomes too great to bear and must be released, often through uncontrollable weeping. This explains why a person in emotional overload may weep at times without apparent reason.

THE FEAR — ADRENALINE CYCLE

I experienced the fear-adrenaline cycle in a terrifying way when burnout struck with gale force. As I felt the waves of anxiety roll over me, the adrenaline rushed into my system, causing even greater fear and anxiety, probably because I was unaware of exactly what was happening. I thought I was "going nuts." Eventually, I learned to simply relax; I began to be thankful that God was in control of His entire creation, instead of trying to fight those awful feelings. As my mind was put to rest because of putting my faith in God, peace would begin to flood my whole being.

IDENTIFYING OUR EMOTIONS

At times in our lives, we all feel negative emotions - depression or worry or anger or hurt or guilt or frustration, or loneliness, to name a few. The first step to taking control of our emotions is to identify what we're *really* feeling inside. Secondly, we must accept the fact that our emotions are calling us to action. Thirdly, we need to realize that we have the power to change direction and take action.

FORMULA FOR SPIRITUAL SUCCESS

If you want to be distressed — look within.

If you want to be defeated — look back.

If you want to be distracted — look around.

If you want to be delivered — look up.

CHAPTER — 8

T*HE GHOSTS OF WORRY,*
FEAR AND ANXIETY

I CAN REMEMBER my mother saying to me as I was *growing up,* **"Worry is like a rocking chair it gives you something to do, but doesn't get you anywhere."**

The swift and sudden descent of depression, along with worry and fear that caught me totally unaware in May 1987, was a shattering experience. I thought to myself *"something must be terribly wrong,"* always the ultimate optimist and a positive thinker, I seldom worried about anything. Now I was terrified that *"now I may lose everything."*

WORRY

The initial sign that stress and unbalanced living had

taken its toll on me mentally was the experience of *worry.* Worry about decisions that had to be made and about financial commitments I had already made usurped the total confidence and faith I had in God and myself. As Vince Lombardi, the great coach once said, *"fatigue makes cowards of us all."*

Worry brought with it waves of anxiety and terrifying thoughts that would leave me in a cold sweat. Burnout brought with it worry, leading to anxiety. From there I spiraled into a state of depression.

The sinking sensation of depression in my stomach robbed me of my appetite. The food I once enjoyed now seemed to have no taste. My stomach felt like an empty pit that wanted to stay that way.

DEPRESSION

Depression also began to rob the desire to recover from burnout. Waking in the morning was the worst time of the day. It brought with it not only another day to face but also the memory of yesterday's suffering. I discovered I needed to get out of bed when I awoke or else my mind would begin to race, putting me into another state of anxiety.

When it comes to our thoughts, I soon realized that the first few waking moments really do set the stage for our entire day. A great way I found to start my day was to jump out of bed and say "This is the day that the Lord has made, I will rejoice and be glad in it." I then began to thank God for all the good things in my life. What a great way to keep depressing thoughts from entering our mind!

Staying off the bed during the day required a great deal of effort but, lying there and continually thinking and worrying in itself is extremely exhausting. Depression was my body's expression of emotional and mental exhaustion.

The thought that depression was a permanent illness kept entering my mind. However, as I was soon to discover, it is only a temporary sickness from which recovery is possible.

Being alone, even traveling to and from work, was tragically depressing for me. During these times, suicidal thoughts would keep entering my mind. I discovered that I needed an organized program of occupation in the presence of others and that time would pass more quickly if my mind was claimed by outside interests.

LIVE ONE DAY AT A TIME

The secret to eliminating worry is to develop the habit of living in "Day-tight Compartments" instead of dwelling on our past failures or worrying about tomorrow. Jesus taught us to pray for today's bread, not tomorrow's. He also said for us not to be anxious about tomorrow.

It appears that worry is a sign of inadequate faith and places self as god.

THE FORMULA FOR SOLVING WORRY

Whenever you are confronted with a situation that tempts you to worry. Simply follow these six steps:

1. Ask yourself *"what is the worst possible thing that could happen in this situation"*.
2. Prepare yourself to accept it, if you have to, by asking yourself these two words *"So what?"*.
3. Calmly decide to improve on the worst case scenario.
4. Before you can improve on the worst case, collect all the facts in a impartial manner. Confusion is the chief cause of worry. Half of your worry may be caused by

trying to make decisions before you have all the facts. Usually in the process of getting the facts, you will find that a problem solves itself.

5. If you've collected all the facts, and the problem still hasn't solved itself, the next step is to analyze the facts and immediately arrive at a decision.

6. Decision without action is useless. The next step is to carry out the decision. Enough thinking, enough investigation, any more thinking will just cause worry and confusion. There comes a time when you must decide to act and never look back.

This formula works every time. Give it a try and watch yourself break free from the habit of worry.

WORRY CAN KILL YOU

Here is a startling fact: more Americans commit suicide each year than die from the five most common communicable diseases. People commit suicide largely because of "Worry-Induced Depression".

Worry can make even the strongest person sick. General Grant discovered this truth in the closing days of the Civil War. The story goes something like this: Grant had been besieging Richmond for nine months. General Lee's troops, ragged and hungry, were beaten. Entire regiments were deserting at a time. Others were holding prayer meetings in their tents — shouting, weeping, and seeing visions. The end was close. Lee's men set fire to the cotton and tobacco warehouses in Richmond, burned the arsenal, and fled from the city at night while towering flames roared up into darkness. Grant was in hot pursuit, banging away at the Confederates from both sides and rear, while Sheridan's cavalry was heading them off in front, tearing up railway lines and capturing supply trains.

Grant, half blind with a violent headache, fell behind his

army and stopped at a farmhouse. *"I spent the night,"* he records in his *Memoirs, "in bathing my feet in hot water and mustard, and putting mustard plasters on my wrists and the back part of my neck, hoping to be cured by morning."*

The next morning he was cured instantaneously. And the thing that cured him was not a mustard plaster, but a horseman galloping down the road with a letter from Lee, saying he wanted to surrender.

"When the officer bearing the message reached me," Grant wrote, *"I was still suffering with the headache, but the instant I saw the note, I was cured."*

It was Grant's worries, tensions and emotions that made him sick. He was cured instantly the moment his emotions took on the hue of confidence, achievement, and victory.

Worry can even put you into a wheelchair with rheumatism and arthritis. Dr. Russel L. Cecil, a world-recognized authority on arthritis, has listed the four most common conditions that bring on arthritis:

1. Marital shipwreck
2. Financial disaster and grief
3. Loneliness and worry
4. Long-cherished resentments

Heart disease is the number-one killer in North America today. During the Second World War, almost a third of a million men were killed in combat, but during the same period, heart disease killed two million civilians-and one million of those casualties were caused by the kind of heart disease brought on by worry-laden and high-tension living. That's probably why Dr. Alexis Carrel said: ***"Businessmen who do not know how to fight worry, die young."***

YOU CAN'T RELAX AND WORRY AT THE SAME TIME

Dr. Israel Bram, a famous specialist in Philadelphia has been treating the worry-related ailment of an acutely overactive thyroid for more than 40 years. People with this condition tremble, they shake, they look like someone scared half to death. Dr. Bram has the following advice painted on a large wooden sign hanging on the wall of his waiting room:

RELAXATION AND WORRY
The most relaxing recreating forces are
a healthy religion, sleep, music, and laughter.
Have faith in God - learn to sleep well -
Love good music - see the funny side of life -
And health and happiness will be yours.

CROWD WORRY OUT OF YOUR MIND

Minds that are not busy tend to be in a vacuum-like state. The remedy for worry is to get busy doing something constructive. Get yourself so busy that you have no time left for worry.

George Bernard Shaw was insightful when he said, ***"The secret of being miserable is to have the leisure to bother about whether or not we are happy or not."*** Lose yourself in action - it's the best medicine.

IF TREES DON'T BEND - THEY BREAK.

It is impossible to live worry-free lives unless we learn to co-operate with the inevitable. When we refuse to accept the inevitable, we set ourselves to be defeated by worry. Like a tree that must bend with the wind or break, we must bend with the inevitable or break mentally.

The philosopher Epictetus taught the Romans nineteen

*centuries ago: **"There is only one way to happiness, and that is to cease worrying about things that are beyond the power of our will."***

DEVELOP AN ATTITUDE OF GRATITUDE

A spirit of thankfulness is usually missing in the lives of those plagued with worry, thankfulness to all those around them and to the God that created all the good things with which He has blessed them. It's very difficult to be truly thankful for today and worry about tomorrow at the same time! Take time every day to thank God for your blessings, your family, your friends, your health, your country, your career, your business. . . . the list goes on.

Dale Carnegie, in his great book *How to Stop Worrying and Start Living*, tells the following story told to him by his friend Harold Abbott. It moved my heart and I trust it will speak to you as well.

"I used to worry a lot," he said, "but one spring day in 1934, I was walking down West Dougherty Street in Webb City when I saw a site that banished all my worries. It all happened in ten seconds, but during those ten seconds, I learned more about how to live than I had learned in the previous ten years. For two years I had been running a grocery store in Webb City," Harold Abbott said as he told Mr. Carnegie the story. *"I had not only lost all my savings, but I had incurred debts that took me seven years to pay back. My grocery store had been closed the previous Saturday; and now I was going to the Merchants and Miners Bank to borrow money so I could go to Kansas City to look for a job. I walked like a beaten man. I had lost all my fight and faith.*

Then suddenly I saw coming down the street a man who had no legs. He was sitting on a little wooden platform equipped with wheels from roller skates. He propelled himself along the street with a block of wood in each hand. I met him just after he had crossed the street and was starting to lift himself up a few inches over the curb to the sidewalk.

As he tilted his little wooden platform to an angle, his eyes met mine. He greeted me with a grand smile. "Good morning, sir. It is a fine morning, isn't it?" he said with spirit. As I stood looking at him, I realized how rich I was. I had two legs. I could walk. I felt ashamed of my self-pity. I said to myself, if he can be happy, cheerful, and confident without legs, I certainly can with legs. I could already feel my chest lifting. I had intended to ask the Merchants and Miners Bank for only one hundred dollars. But now I had courage to ask for two hundred. I had intended to say that I wanted to go to Kansas City to try to get a job. But now I announced confidently that I wanted to go to Kansas City to get a job. I got the loan; and I got the job.

"I now have the following words pasted on my bathroom mirror, and I read them every morning as I shave:

I had the blues because I had no shoes,

Until upon the street, I met a man who had no feet."

WORRY PREVENTION

Probably the most important factor in worry prevention is the prevention of fatigue. I have found in my own life that when I'm worn-out physically, I am susceptible to worry. Much like the way fatigue lowers our resistance to the common cold, fatigue lowers our resistance to the emotions of fear and worry.

The first rule of worry prevention is simple: **Rest before you get tired**. Plan and take your next vacation before you need it.

The second rule for worry prevention is: **Learn to relax.** Since it is not our brain that tires from mental work, we need only to focus on relaxing our muscles in order to prevent fatigue. The Metropolitan Life Insurance Company points this out in a leaflet on fatigue: "Hard work by itself seldom causes fatigue which cannot be cured by a good sleep or rest. Worry, tenseness, and emotional upset are three of the biggest causes of fatigue. Often they are to blame when physical or mental work seems to be the cause. Remember that a tense muscle is a working muscle. Ease up! Save energy for the important duties." So, the next time you are sitting at your desk, feeling tired and stressed-out, sit back, close your eyes and begin speaking silently to your muscles, telling them to relax. Start with your toes and work your way up your body, paying special attention to the jaw muscles where we store much of our nervous tension. It is also very important to relax our eye muscles since they burn up one fourth of all the nervous energies consumed by the body.

The third worry prevention rule is this: **Get enough physical exercise in the open air.** Without becoming physically exhausted at something other than work at least three times a week, we all run the risk of developing worry habits. Work yourself into a good sweat and you'll see that worry and depression will ooze out your body with the sweat. Physical activity is absolutely vital in any worry prevention program.

Dr. Link in his book, *The Rediscovery of Man,* writes about a patient who wanted to commit suicide. Dr. Link knew that arguing would only make matters worse, so he said to the man, *"If you are going to commit suicide anyway, you might as well do it in a heroic fashion. Run around the block until you drop dead."*

He tried it, not once but several times, and each time he felt better in his mind if not in his muscles. By the third night, he had achieved what Dr. Link intended in the first place - he was so physically tired (and physically relaxed) that he slept like a log. Later he joined an athletic club and began to compete in competitive sports. Soon he was feeling so good that he wanted to live forever.

The fourth rule of worry prevention is clear: **Develop good working habits.** Good working habits can only be developed by planning and organizing your day in advance. Be certain that you expend energy only on those tasks which take you closer to your goals. Prioritize your tasks. Focus on only one task at a time until it is complete. Spend some time every day reviewing your progress towards you goals. In other words "Plan - Do - And then Review" making small adjustments to your course every day.

The fifth worry prevention rule is vital: **Live life with a passion.** If you can't get passionate about your work, perhaps it's time for a career change. If you can't get passionate about your play time, perhaps it's time for a new hobby. If you can't get passionate about anything, perhaps it's time for an attitude adjustment. People who are passionate about life spend it with people who are the same. They begin their day with the decision to give it all they've got. They're going to go big or stay home!

The Five Ways to Prevent Worry:

1. Rest before you get tired.

2. Learn to relax.

3. Get plenty of physical exercise.

4. Develop good working habits.

5. Get passionate about life.

"Worry is the interest paid on a debt you may not owe."

FEAR

"Fear is the main source of superstition, and one of the main sources of cruelty. To conquer fear is the beginning of wisdom."

- BERTRAND RUSSEL

CHAPTER — 9

HOW TO BEAT DEPRESSION AND LIVE AGAIN

THE ILLNESS OF DEPRESSION.

Depression is a sickness that we can trace right back to biblical times when we read about Job, who lost fortune and family and was afflicted with boils covering his body. Who wouldn't be depressed in those circumstances?

Today over 75,000 people a year commit suicide in North America. Investigations reveal that over half of these victims were suffering from depression. Add to that the fact that only a small percentage who attempt suicide actually succeed.

Depression seems to be a universal illness that most of us have experienced to some degree in life. We all seem to be susceptible, regardless of position, possessions or popularity. I have met depressed accountants, housewives, pastors, construction workers and businessmen. Even Sir Winston Churchill was given to severe bouts of depression and yet was a great leader at a time of national crisis. Some of the world's greatest men were plagued with this problem and would fall into a period of depression after some outstanding accomplishment. It seems they had just run out of goals, just as I had. There are, however, other causes of depression. Here is a list of a few:

1. The number-one cause of depression is the lack of clearly defined long-term goals. It is also important to note that it is quite normal to experience depression soon after you have achieved a worthy goal, but before you've taken time to set another goal.

2. Depression is also caused by looking inward instead of being focused on helping others. Becoming involved with local charities as a volunteer is a great way to beat the blahs. Helping others in need, makes us forget we need help ourselves. I have traveled around the world helping those in need and can tell you that there is nothing as uplifting as helping another human being.

3. Another cause of depression is a chemical imbalance in our bodies. Sometimes this is caused by a lack of physical exercise, and at other times, it is a hereditary thing, at still other times, it is some traumatic experience in our past.

4. We become what we read and watch the most. The media pumps negativity into our minds because that's what sells their newspapers and gets their TV ratings up. Perhaps that's why the top CEO's only watch an average of five hours of TV per week when the average North American watches five times as much.

We become what we think about the most.

5. Being around some people is a depressing experience in itself. Negative people can get positive people down a lot easier than the other way around. To be happy and positive, it's absolutely necessary to surround ourselves with happy and positive people.

6. Negative self-talk will cause depression. Our subconscious mind receives self-talk messages at the rate of 1200 words per minute. That's twenty words every second. It's easy to see how we can talk ourselves up or down very quickly at that rate.

It's amazing how happy some people can be amidst some of life's saddest experiences. Their joy just continues to radiate, while others seem to find a reason to be depressed over joyful circumstances. Recovery from depression is only possible when we realize that it is our attitude toward circumstances, not the circumstances themselves that cause us to be depressed.

SYMPTOMS OF DEPRESSION:

Emotional

1. Fear, worry and anxiety

   Somehow we find reason to worry about all the things we can't change. The exciting challenges in our lives now appear to us as problems and potential failures. Our faith turns to fear and anxiety takes over our trust in God.

2. Irritability

   When we are depressed, we will become irritated very easily. Coming home after a long day's work, we find that the noise caused by the family we love can irritate to no end. The people we work with and the customers we serve see us as irritable, edgy and hard to get along with, instead of the loving, kind and considerate person they once knew.

3. Lack of Joy

    With depression comes an immediate lack of joy or happiness. Forcing a smile requires a great deal of effort. However, the forced smile serves as a poor mask for the emotional pain written across the face of a depressed person. We pretend to be happy, but unless we are happy inside, we look miserable on the outside. Things that once brought happiness now bring no joy whatsoever.

4. Crying

    When we are depressed, we often tend to cry involuntarily. Weeping and depression seem to go hand in hand. Weeping seems to be our means of releasing the pent-up emotions and feelings from our minds as depression sets in.

5. Despair

    We are overcome with feelings of hopelessness. There appears to be no end in sight to our suffering, no light at the end of the tunnel. To the patient, this sickness seems to be terminal.

PHYSICAL

1. Chronic Fatigue

    When depressed, we tend to wake up tired and continue to feel tired all day long. We don't even enjoy our hobbies. It feels as though someone opened a tap and drained all the energy out of our bodies. Sleep seems to no longer re-vitalize us or re-store our energy levels. Our bodies feel as though they need to be dragged around. The zeal and zest for life are gone.

2. Insomnia

    It is common when we are depressed to have difficulty falling asleep, although some of us oversleep and still awake tired. Lying there and waiting for sleep to come as our mind speeds on can cause a great deal of anxiety in itself. Our body is resting, but our mind refuses to stop thinking and worrying. There are times we fall asleep only to awake a short time later in a cold sweat. Prescribed sedatives can be a real lifesaver without causing an addiction.

3. Unkept Appearance

    Our clothes reveal a great deal about the kind of image we hold of ourselves. I've seen men who have awoken depressed and shown up at work unshaven, their hair a mess and their clothes looking like they slept in them. We portray how we feel on the inside by the way we look on the outside. How we look is generally how we feel, yet it requires the same energy to dress up as it does to dress down.

4. Appetite

    Food seems to lose its taste. The stomach feels tied in a knot as our appetite for food disappears. Some people, however, begin to overeat and totally neglect their diets. After all, when we were kids, our parents used to give us a treat or a snack to make us feel better if we were crying.

5. Physical Ailments

    Even though these ailments are sometimes imagined, depressed people experience chest pains, headaches, respiratory problems and weakness. These are actually symptoms of the stress that caused our depression.

THE CHARACTERISTICS OF THREE KINDS OF DEPRESSION

	Discourage-ment (mild)	Despondency (serious)	Despair (severe)
Mental	Self-doubt	Self-criticism	Self-rejection
	Resentment	Anger	Bitterness
	Self-pity	Self-pity	Self-pity
Physical	Loss of appetite	Apathy	Withdrawal
	Sleeplessness	Hypochon-dria	Passivity
	Unkept appearance	"Weeps"	Catatonia
Emotional	Discontent	Distress	Hopelessness
	Sadness	Sorrow	Schizophrenia
	Irritability	Loneliness	Abandonment
Spiritual	Question God's will	Resentment to God's will	Anger at God's will

As devastating as depression may be, there is hope for recovery, regardless of how awful you may be feeling. The secret to recovery lies in the next chapter.

The Manic Depressive

Manic-depressive, or bi-polar illness, is a term used by psychiatrists to describe those people who, one moment are at the top of the world and the next, are in the depths' of despair. They spend little time on base line. During their highs, they are super-creative, they are very productive, they laugh and talk, and are fun to be around. These people are also prone to be compulsive spenders and sometimes have uncontrollable sexual desires when they are at the top of their emotional cycle.

However, when these folks are down, look out. They can be miserable to be around, for they become inefficient at their jobs and can't see any reason to continue living and become suicidal. Depression may seem like a negative topic to study or discuss, but understanding this illness is important. Being able to recognize the symptoms in the early stages and knowing how to take remedial action are the first steps toward experiencing a life of consistent joy and peace in spite of circumstances.

Religious people experiencing depression may feel that God has forsaken them or that the devil is tempting them. That's simply because religion in the abstract is only form. Form is no substitute for a personal relationship with our Creator. Putting our faith in God and believing He is in control should be our support as we patiently watch our body heal as our mind finds peace.

If you have a loved one going through depression please be patient, but that doesn't mean you need to be too sympathetic. Misery loves company. Merely listening to and sympathizing with the patient won't do either of you any good.

WHEN IT LOOKS LIKE I HAVE FAILED

Lord, are you trying to tell me something?

For . . . .

Failure does not mean I'm a failure;

It does mean I have not yet succeeded.

Failure does not mean I have accomplished nothing;

It does mean I have learned something.

Failure does not mean I have been a fool;

It does mean I had enough faith to experiment.

Failure does not mean I've been disgraced,

It does mean I dared to try.

Failure does not mean I don't have it;

It does mean I have to do something in a different way.

Failure does not mean I am inferior;

It does mean I am not perfect.

Failure does not mean I've wasted my time;

It does mean I have an excuse to start over.

Failure does not mean I should give up;

It does mean I have to try harder.

Failure does not mean I'll never make it,

It does mean I need more patience.

Failure does not mean you have abandoned me;

It does mean you must have a better idea. Amen.

– Author Unknown

CHAPTER — 10

TIME OUT!

SHARPENING THE SAW

It has always been a challenge to incorporate leisure and rest into my life. Like the majority of people, I worked so that I could take a vacation; I did not take a vacation so that I could work. In other words, I never thought of taking a vacation to renew myself so that I could return to work with a restored passion. In this sense, taking a vacation is like sharpening the saw.

Before burnout, I would spend a week or two a year on vacation with my family. During a visit to my family doctor, while I was experiencing burnout, he recommended I take my family on a vacation. *"It needs to be for an indefinite period of time, and you should return only when you have recovered mentally and are eager to return to your business."* I took the vacation, and it did the trick. I was on the road to recovery. In three weeks, I was back to work and feeling one hundred percent better. My energy had returned, and my depression had lifted.

The doctor also recommended that, for the future, I take a two week vacation every three months or a ten day vacation every ten weeks. Since that suggestion in 1987, I have spent six to eight weeks on vacation most years. I believe these saw-sharpening breaks have been the most vital part of my burnout prevention program since recovery.

Many people ask me *"How can a person with only a 2 week per year vacation entitlement stay sharp?"* The answer is that some jobs don't require more than two weeks vacation a year to prevent burnout. These are low-stress jobs. A weekend is an adequate break to recuperate from the previous five days of stress.

THE INNER WARNING BELL

We have all, at one time or another, heard a warning bell go off inside us. Overwhelming feelings of fatigue, unhappiness, anxiety or self-doubt are warning signals for us to step back, reevaluate and change the direction of our life. Most of us have heard our inner coach signaling for *time out.* However, we are all the referees of our own lives; it's up to us to blow the whistle and stop the game. Sadly, we often ignore the signals from our *inner coach.*

For those of us who don't heed the first signal from our *inner coach*, and keep right on playing, the coach must send a stronger signal, like a slap upside the head. For some, that slap is a heart attack, for some, it's burnout and, for some, it's suicide. We get carried out of the game on a stretcher.

RENEWAL

Human energy is a renewal resource. The problem is that too many people think they can run on empty. God has given each one of us the free gift of energy to burn, not to be stored, but to be used for our own good and for the good of others. Like any other natural resource we use, if energy is not restored, it is soon depleted. What an awesome principle.

The "Low Fuel" warning lights built into each one of us are like those of an airplane. If the pilot ignores the fuel gauge and the "Low Fuel" warning lights, and keeps on flying, the plane will eventually run out of fuel and crash. Even though some aircraft can refuel in-flight, all must land for maintenance or eventually crash. Renewal means stopping for fuel and maintenance before we crash. Recovery means stopping for repair after we crash.

HOW TO TAKE A BREAK

Don't wait too long. Some people need a reason for everything, and thus don't take a vacation until they desperately need one - when they are physically exhausted, burned-out, or ill. The best time to plan your next vacation is before you return home from the vacation you are currently enjoying.

Don't expect too much. The anticipation of your next holiday is as beneficial as the holiday itself. However, a vacation itself can sometimes be stressful, especially if we've set our expectations too high and things don't measure up.

Don't overplan. I know people who have every hour of their vacation planned before they leave home. They leave no room for spontaneity, no time for the unexpected. Is it any wonder they return from their vacations as uptight as when they left?

Don't overdo. Leisure means rest opportunity, unhurried quietude, relaxation, calm, reprieve. Now, think of your last vacation. How much time did you spend resting, relaxing, in quietness? How much time did you spend in solitude?

Make a list of vacation goals. Try picking up a travel brochure and clipping out a picture of that place you would like to visit. Pin it up where you will see it frequently, and you will be amazed at how quickly you will be taking that vacation.

Take a mini vacation. Take an extra day on a long weekend and make it a mini vacation. Three and four day vacations are becoming very popular in 90's. Even though it may take on the average twenty-four to forty-eight hours to unwind, the body is able to rejuvenate rapidly in a state of rest.

SLOW ME DOWN, LORD

Slow me down, Lord.

Ease the pounding of my heart by the quieting of my mind.

Steady my hurried pace with a vision of the eternal reach of time.

Give me, amid the confusion of the day, the calmness of the everlasting hills.

Break the tensions of my nerves and the muscles with the soothing music of the singing streams that live in my memory.

Teach me the art of taking minute vacations - of slowing down to look at a flower, to chat with a friend, to pat a dog, to smile at a child, to read a few lines from a good book.

Remind me each day that the race is not always to the swift; that there is more to life than increasing its speed.

Let me look upward to the towering oak and know that it grew great and strong because it grew slowly and well.

– Rev. Wilfred A. Peterson

CHAPTER — 11

BALANCED GOAL SETTING

GOAL-SETTING CAN be the most creative, and at the same time, the most destructive force in our lives. It is a creative force when our goals are balanced and our motives are right, but imbalanced goals set with selfish motives can destroy our family, our health and our soul. The dictionary describes a goal as "an aim or purpose." We need to pursue challenging goals for every area of our lives in order to experience a sense of total well being and balance.

Before burnout, my goals revolved entirely around finances and myself. I had three areas in my life in which I had set goals. The first was the business/finance area, and I can't remember the other two. The world viewed me as super-successful because all I touched seemed to turn into gold and any goal I set I seemed to achieve. I was a winner, and there wasn't a project or business I would start that didn't become a success. The fact was, that I had only set goals for one area in my life. I was no more successful than my heroes, Robert Campeau and Donald Trump, who had amassed great wealth as real-estate developers but destroyed their health, family or soul in the process.

I discovered, however, that there is another option. This option would allow me to experience health, wealth, family, recreation and a spiritual relationship with my God all at the same time and in a perfect balance. This option is called balanced goal-setting for balanced living. It's joy. It's bliss. It's heaven on earth. It comes with a list of standard features most people would consider options:

- Health, love and leisure.
- Peace, joy and contentment.
- Wisdom, strength and self-confidence.
- Success, wealth and abundance.

Life is meant to be lived and expressed with enthusiasm, joy and a peace of mind that is far beyond explanation. Helen Keller once said, *"Life is either a daring adventure or nothing."* I agree!

WHY SET GOALS ANYWAY?

My brother Pete is an avid hunter and a good shot with the crossbow. I have never shot the crossbow but, I know that with ten minutes of practice I could out-shoot Pete with one hand tied behind my back, provided he was blindfolded first. You can't hit a target you can't see! You can't reach a goal you haven't set. It's like reaching a destination you don't have or coming back from a place you have never been. Traveling 70 miles an hour is efficient, but going the right direction is effective. A person without a goal is like a ship without a rudder. Both will drift aimlessly and accomplish little.

Many people just go with the flow, following each other to work and home every day like a bunch of processionary caterpillars. They never make it to becoming a butterfly and experience real freedom; instead, they die of starvation as a caterpillar following a procession called "the masses" in a circle that goes nowhere. As butterflies, we are able to fly over the obstacles and problems that once stopped us when we were crawling on our bellies as caterpillars. Because of our altitude as a butterfly, our vision improves and our goals are easier to reach.

Average North Americans spend more time planning their vacations than they spend planning the rest of their lives. Is it any wonder that the majority lack enthusiasm, motivation and direction in their lives? Why set goals?

- Goals help keep our attention focused on an objective and our purpose in life.

- They give us energy and enthusiasm. They flip on the switch that allows the current to flow. The power to accomplish becomes reality.

- Goals make us more efficient and productive. They help us stop wasting our time with things that are not important.

- Goals chart a course for our lives to follow. They give us a road map to follow and make us effective. People with goals succeed because they know where they're heading.

- Goals help us manage our time. NOT TRUE! Time can't be managed. We can only manage ourselves. People complaining about lack of time are usually saying they lack direction.

- Goal-setting is a rewarding and fulfilling experience. We can't experience achievement without goals.

ZIG ZIGLAR

As one of my mentors Zig Ziglar, a motivational speaker and author, says *"With goals we become a meaningful specific instead of a wandering generality."* Reading his book *See You At The Top* is a life-changing experience. After I read it for the first time (books like these, need to be re-read many times), I discovered I had found my mentor at last. If I had read his book ten years earlier and had lived it, I'm certain I wouldn't be writing a book today (from experience) on the subject of burnout.

True happiness can only be achieved by living a balanced life. Living a balanced life is only possible with written, long-term, balanced goals for every area of our lives.

Setting goals is harder than reaching them. However, since we can't reach a goal we haven't set, goal-setting does come before the reaching. A great goal-setting tool I've come upon and use, is a book by Mark Victor Hansen called — *Future Diary.* It will explain the step-by-step process of writing virtually dozens of goals for every area of our life. Another book that has been a tremendous help to me in establishing a balance in goal-setting is *Success! The Glenn Bland Method*, by Glenn Bland. He demonstrates how to set goals and make plans that really work. They did for me!

J. C. Penny once said *"Give me a stockclerk with a goal and I will give you a man who will make history. Give me a man without a goal, and I will give you a stockclerk."*

HOW DO WE SET OUR GOALS?

Goals must be written and reviewed regularly. Only three percent of all people set goals and write them down. Ten percent have plans and goals but keep them in their heads. The three percent of people with written goals accomplish from fifty to one hundred times more during their life time than the ten percent with their goals only in their heads. A goal is only a dream until it is written down. Setting goals is practically free. All you need to do is take a pen and pad and start writing. Don't limit your imagination!

Be specific with your goals as well as your prayers. Don't expect anything you don't desire and don't desire anything you don't expect. Set your goals with a deadline. This creates a little pressure but certainly makes us more productive.

We need to set long-range goals to help us overcome the short-term obstacles we may face. As we step out with the faith we already have and go as far as we can see, when we get there, we'll see farther and will have acquired more faith to continue. Long-term goals demand a daily commitment to action and must be reinforced by a regular review of objectives and accomplishments.

TYPES OF GOALS

In order to set our goals in a balanced fashion, you need to categorize them in a way that is meaningful and easy to relate to in your everyday life. Use the spaces provided below each category to list some of your own goals. We all need short-term goals (the next 6 months), mid-term goals (within 6-12 months), long-term goals (during the next 2-5 years), and lifetime goals (those things we wish to accomplish within our lifetime). Start now!

1. SPIRITUAL GOALS.

a.) Spiritual Development Goals
- prayer time
- meditation
- bible study
- church attendance
- empowering and enriching others

b.) Habit-breaker Goals
- smoking
- alcohol and drug abuse
- profane language

2. FINANCIAL GOALS

Make all you can, save all you can, give all you can.

a.) Career/Business Goals
- getting a raise
- getting a promotion
- starting my own business
- business growth

b.) Earning Goals
- my annual earnings this year
- my annual earnings next year

- my annual earnings in five years
- **c.) Saving Goals**
  - real-estate investments
  - retirement savings
  - bank account balanced
- **d.) Giving Goals**
  - tithing
  - contributing my time
  - giving to the poor

3. RECREATIONAL GOALS

Come away before you come apart.
- **a.) Exercise Goals**
  - walking
  - swimming
  - jogging
- **b.) Hobby Goals**
  - gardening
  - horseback riding
  - golfing
- **c.) Sports Goals**
  - golfing
  - squash
  - baseball
  - hockey

4. FAMILY GOALS

Time spent with the family is high priority time.
- **a.) Spouse Goals**
  - daily shared time
  - weekly date
  - yearly honeymoon
- **b.) Children Goals**
  - daily play time with children

- devotional times
- educational times

c.) **Parent Goals**
- time shared with parents
- remembering their special days

5. MENTAL GOALS

As a man thinketh, so he is.

a.) **Educational Goals**
- books that I will read
- tapes I will listen to
- courses I will take
- languages I will learn

b.) **Emotional Goals**
- outwardly express my appreciation of others
- hug twelve people every day

c.) **Thought Goals**
- think positive thoughts
- reject every thought that is negative or impure

6. HEALTH GOALS

"We become what we eat."
- my diet
- my daily exercise
- my physical weight and shape
- my sleep routine

7. SOCIAL GOALS

It's not what you know, it's whom you know.
- the people I will meet
- the friends I will make
- entertaining

8.   CHARACTER GOALS

Your reputation is who people think you are, your character is who you really are.

- integrity
- honesty
- meekness
- charity
- love

DO WE TELL ANYONE OUR GOALS?

There is a general tendency for us to conceal our goals. That way, just in case we don't achieve them, no one will know. No one will ever say *"Hey Ben, whatever happened to that book you said you were going to write?"* or *"How is your weight-loss program doing?"* On the other hand, how can the crowd cheer if they don't know where the finish line is? How can they applaud the scoring of a goal, when our game has invisible nets? Fans will support their home-team if they know that they are playing a game. Keep the game a secret and see how many people show up!

Before I began this book I told at least a hundred people that I was about to write a book, even though I had never done it before. I also didn't know how I would find the time. Since that time, countless people have asked me *"How's the book coming?"* Sometimes I wished I hadn't told anyone about my goal of writing a book. However, here I am, half way through. It is important to share your goals and dreams with those who love and support you and want to see you succeed.   Call these people your *Accountability Team* or your *Board of Advisors*, whatever, they represent a great opportunity to share your goals and get tremendous support.

THE MASTERMIND PRINCIPLE

A *Mastermind Team* is a group of like-minded individuals (usually 2-6 people) meeting regularly for an hour to share their goals, ideas and skills. They hold the team leader accountable by asking the hard questions, like "What have you been doing lately to bring you closer to reaching your goals?"... "How are you doing with integrity and honesty?"..."How is your balance?" Each member of the group makes a commitment to support all the other members of the group in their goals and dreams and contribute any skills or contacts they have. Every person in the group must be loving, giving and positive in attitude. A single negative person can totally destroy the harmony of a group.

As we share ideas and challenge each other's mental abilities, we grow mentally and spiritually. As we share our energy, ideas and skills with the others in the group, we experience an explosion in our own strength and mental power. Once again, we see how the law of giving works.

When we are involved in an accountability relationship and are in rapport with others, we become more aware that there is strength in numbers. A single arrow can easily be broken, but grab a handful of them and you will notice that they are virtually unbreakable.

Andrew Carnegie and other great individuals in the past have used accountability and masterminding very successfully. By ourselves, none of us can be truly successful, since we all need inspiration, encouragement and accountability. The fallen leaders of recent past are a clear indication that standing alone is a dangerous position, especially so, if we are at the top. We need that circle of support and protection called the "accountability team" around us as a shield against the destructive arrows of imbalanced goals, selfish motives, mediocrity and complacency.

Think as big as you dare, when you formulate your goals and begin to write them down. Some wise human being once said, *"It is better to aim your arrow at a star and hit an eagle, then to aim your arrow at an eagle and hit a stone."* Set **BIG** goals. We need goals that are big enough to excite us and high enough to make us reach.

As Booker T. Washington said, *"You measure the size of the accomplishment by the obstacles you have to overcome to reach your goals."*

Every day, you should review your goals and take steps towards them. Set your goals with proper motives in mind. It is amazing how much stress is eliminated when our goals are unselfish and our motives are pure. I believe God wants to bless us and help us prosper so we can be a blessing to others and help them prosper. Our cups need to be full and running over with abundance in order to meet the needs of others effectively. No individual can attain true riches unless he is willing to enrich the lives of others around him.

IT'S UP TO YOU!

If you think you are a winner you'll win,

If you dare to step out you will succeed.

Believe in your heart, have a purpose to start.

Aim to help fellow man in his need.

Thoughts of faith must replace every doubt.

Use words of courage and you cannot fail.

If you stumble and fall, rise and stand ten feet tall

You determine the course that you sail.

For in life as in death, don't you see,

It's the man who has nothing to fear

Who approaches the gates, stands a moment and waits.

Feels the presence of God oh so near.

You've been given the power to see

What it takes to be a real person.

Let your thinking be pure, it will make you secure.

If you want to, you know that you can.

– Author Unknown

CHAPTER — 12

FARM TALK... THE LAW OF THE HARVEST

IT'S LIVE!!!

I had no idea that afternoon as I knelt on the edge of a two-storey building, that   seconds later I would be traveling towards the ground head first. I also had no idea that the high voltage ballast I was changing was live! As my apprentice (my brother Jamie) handed me a wire he had just disconnected, he began to say *"Watch it, it's live!"* It was too late! Electricity jolted through my body propelling me towards a large shrub on the ground below. I did a somersault on the way down, landing on my feet and flattening the shrub, spraining both ankles and cracking two vertebrae. That's the law of gravity for you. It works every time!

The law of the harvest began to take on new meaning to me as I began to reap the results of seven years of imbalanced living. The law of the harvest is the same as the law of gravity in that, whether you believe in it or not, it still operates. This same idea will apply to all of the success principles discussed in this book. They are in operation whether or not we believe they are. You will understand the reason for failures in certain areas of your life when you get a handle on the law of harvest. You will also perhaps realize why some people are successful and others are not, yet both have the same resources at their disposal. I also believe that the more principle-centered we become, the less we use the word luck.

The law of the harvest is found in Galations 6:7 ***"Be not deceived, God is not mocked: For whatsoever a man soweth, that shall he also reap."***

Being raised on a farm, I had the privilege of watching first-hand, the amazing process of planting and harvest. What always amazed me was placing seeds into the ground and observing the little plants shoot up and mature into a beautiful golden crop of grain ready for harvest. As harvest would begin, there was an air of excitement; everyone was anxious to see the fruits of their labor being brought in. I would seize every opportunity to ride the combine and watch in awe as the stalks of grain disappeared into the throat of the gigantic machine and then reappeared in the bin to the rear as clean grain. Those few seeds we had planted in the spring had miraculously been transformed into a bountiful harvest. We were harvesting the same type of crop we had planted. Because we had planted, we would have food to eat for another winter.

IT WORKS EVERY TIME!

Witnessing as a youth the miracle of planting in order to harvest, I began to experience the same law at work in my own personal life. As I studied the lives of both successful people and those who seem to be losers, I discovered that the law of the harvest is universal and timeless. It has no respect for age, financial status or religious belief. It can be our greatest asset or our greatest liability. We get to choose the seeds we plant into our minds, the soil of our lives.

Let me share with you some observations of my own with regard to the planting and reaping of crops and how the law of the farm applies to our personal lives.

The Seven Laws Of The Harvest

1.   You pick what you plant.
2.   You always plant before you pick.
3.   You perish before you prosper.
4.   You have to work at weeding.
5.   Patience pays off.
6.   It's rough before you reap.
7.   Perpetual planting equals repeated reaping.

Let's look at how the seven laws of the harvest apply to our lives. They determine whether we reap a bountiful crop of happiness, love and material abundance or a crop of weeds (misery, anxiety, depression, and greed).

1. You pick what you plant.

In other words, don't plant anything you wouldn't want to harvest. This idea seems to be so obvious. Yet it comes as a surprise to most people who have been consumed by a career or business for years to discover they have lost their family and their soul in the process. They treat people dishonestly and wonder why others cheat them. They are tightwads with their money and can't figure out why they never have enough to make ends meet. What goes around, comes around!

They eat junk foods and fail to get proper exercise and wonder why they have heart attacks, become obese or lack energy and enthusiasm. A regular vacation seems like a waste of time, so weekends are spent working, eventually when their bodies become sick to give them rest, it's a surprise! They abuse their bodies with tobacco and are shocked to discover they have cancer.

Our mind will also only grow the kind of crops that are planted in it. If we plant a seed of doubt, we will reap a crop of fear. If we plant a seed of fear, we will reap a crop of the very thing we fear. As Job said, "The very thing I feared, has come upon me." However, if we plant the seed of faith, we can expect to reap the very thing in which we believe. Too often we say *"I'll believe it when I see it,"* when really, *"we'll only see it if we believe it."*

We also reap in direct proportion to the amount of seed we have sown. Abundant harvesting requires abundant sowing. If you want a hug, you need to give a hug away. Want a friend? Be a friend. If you would like your financial needs abundantly met, freely give to those in need. Want to be happy? Make someone else happy! Your harvest is determined at the time of planting, not at the time of harvest. A farmer decides in the spring what crop it is he would like to harvest later that year. He cannot change his mind and harvest a crop he did not plant.

So it is in our personal lives. Our future depends on the seeds we are planting today. If we want the love and respect from our kids when they are teenagers or adults, we must give them our time and effort today. After we have become a financial success and they have gone off to live their own lives, it may be too late.

We would all like to be treated with caring affection and regard in our senior years. We must therefore, reach out to the elderly with love in our youth and expect to reap what we have sown.

Enjoying a healthy body in the future, will be determined by how we look after our bodies today. The alcoholic can count on reaping poor health and family problems. I have friends today who are coping with physical ailments that are a result of an alcohol addiction they had twenty years ago. I also know families that are broken today because of the damage caused in the past by an alcoholic parent.

Burnout occurs when we sow the seeds of workaholism and gross imbalance in our lives, fertilize them with greed, fear and anxiety and harvest the results of depression, anxiety and despair.

2. You always plant before you pick.

The seeds we plant in our lives symbolize the goals we have set for our lives. As we discover balanced goal setting later on this book, we will see how goals begin in our heads but, must then be felt in our hearts. We still have only a dream until our goal is put into writing. Writing our goals is planting our seeds.

Our actions are all a direct results of the seeds of thought we have planted in our past. The same applies to any harvest. The planting of the seed must take place first. Good crops can only be harvested if good seeds were first planted. However, too many people expect a harvest without planting any seeds. They plan to plant after they have harvested enough to satisfy all their needs. They will start to give to charities after they have paid off the mortgage and have put the kids through college. They will begin volunteering their time once they're not so busy with their careers or businesses. They'll be a friend after you become one first to them. They will be more positive once their situation improves. They will work harder and longer and take more responsibility after they receive that raise in pay. Get the picture? To think we can harvest before planting makes no sense at all!

The keys to a successful harvest are; first, to plan your crop — dream your dreams; second, to prepare the soil — define the resources required to reach your goals; third, to plant the seed — write down your goals; fourth, to maintain the soil — guard you thoughts; last, to expect a crop.

Winners plan to win; they prepare to win and they expect to win.

3. You perish before you prosper.

When a farmer places that seed into the soil he has carefully prepared for it, he is taking a great risk. He plants with the expectation of harvest, knowing he can't retrieve the seed, should it not germinate. He simply plants, knowing that the seed will die but at the same time believing new life will then spring forth. The sower takes the risk and plants the seed, but he cannot make it grow. We need to take the risk but believe for the results.

This law works exactly the same way in our lives. As we reach out and touch the lives of people around us, we take a risk. Sowing seeds of love and affection, we invest greatly, and risk never seeing that love returned by the person we may be helping at the time. After we've done our part ... sometimes all we can do is believe. Like the farmer, if we just keep on planting in faith, we will eventually reap. Our faith in God is the moisture required to achieve germination. It takes great faith to plant something that must die and we may never see again, but the risk is worth the rewards. Without death, there is no life. Without the possibility of loss, there could be no win. Without valleys, there could be no mountains. Without sorrow, there would be no joy!

FAILURE IS THE FERTILIZER OF ACHIEVEMENT

When crop failures come, (and they will), they are only meant to be faith builders. They make us better, stronger and wiser. There are no failures in life - only learning experiences. Failures can be turned into fertilizer or a deadly chemical that destroys our lives. The choice is ours!

Think about these people:

- Henry Ford failed and went broke five times before he finally succeeded.
- Walt Disney was fired by a newspaper editor for a lack of ideas. Walt Disney also went bankrupt several times before he built Disneyland.
- Babe Ruth, famous for setting the home run record and one of the greatest athletes of all time, also holds the record for strikeouts.

4. You have to work at weeding.

As a child, I can remember farmers giving land a rest periodically. This practice is not very common today, but instead of planting a crop every year, they would simply cultivate it all summer to keep the weeds from growing and going to seed. This process is called "summer-fallow." No seeds have been planted, yet the weeds seem to grow as though they had been planted by an unseen hand.

This process appears to take place as well in our own lives and, unless we are continually sowing and cultivating the seeds of love, the weeds of envy and hate will begin to grow. Constantly feeding our minds with positive information will prevent the negativism from sprouting and shooting up, bearing a crop of weeds. Unless we're making a positive impact on our families by sowing into their lives the seeds of caring, sharing and leading by example, we can be sure that their lives will bear a bountiful crop of weeds.

We are what we are because of what has gone into our minds in the past, the people we've met and the influence those people have had on our lives. Positive, happy, successful people feed their minds with that which is uplifting, positive, good and pure. They also choose to associate themselves with other people that are positive and prosperous. This is planting good seeds.

People who have failed miserably at life have fed their minds with bad news and negative self-talk. They love to talk about their problems and those of others. They love to criticize and put down, instead of building up their fellow worker. The seeds they plant are weed seeds. Is it any wonder they only reap crops of weeds?

Crops require maintenance — weeds don't. Without weed control, most farmers wouldn't have much of a crop. Weeds grow faster and are hardier than the crop we've planted. I can remember as a boy spending part of the summer walking through the grain fields pulling a weed called *wild mustard.*

In my life, I think of weed seeds as the negative

thoughts that want to keep planting themselves into my mind. If these negative thoughts are not rejected immediately, they begin to choke out the good, happy and positive thoughts. An act repeated for twenty one to thirty days becomes a *habit*. This period of time appears to be the gestation period for a habit.

Maintenance requires continually monitoring our motives, desires and needs. Weeding our garden means going through it and deciding which plants are weeds, then pulling them out by the roots so that they can no longer grow. Weeding our minds is the same process; however, instead of weeding plants, we must weed out our critical, negative thoughts.

Maintenance also requires the fertilizing of our good, pure, positive thoughts with a regular daily review of our goals, reading good books and listening to tapes that inspire, motivate and educate while we are driving.

5. Patience pays off.

This principle applies to both good seeds and bad. It took seven years of burning the candle at both ends before it got so hot in the middle that I burnt out. It also took six months of applying balanced living principles before I really noticed a significant change in my physical, mental and spiritual condition. I did, however, experience a positive change in my condition before the six months, but the "up times" didn't last long and were followed by periods of depression.

Likewise, the abuse of our bodies with alcohol, tobacco, drugs, lack of exercise, a poor diet or workaholism during youth is the reason many people spend their so-called *"golden years"* in poor health. After spending a lifetime working towards retirement, they arrive only to find misery, boredom and sickness.

Unwittingly, many people exchange a full and long life for a few years of the *"good times,"* (if you can call abuse of our bodies "good times") followed by sickness and premature death.

The Chinese bamboo takes four years of cultivation before there are any signs of life. During that period of time the farmer weeds, waters and waits. During the fifth year, in a six week period the Chinese Bamboo grows 90 feet. If the farmer gave up before the fifth year, he wouldn't have a crop to harvest. Bamboo farming, like life, takes determination, patience, and stick-to-itive-ness.

It may take a while, but we always reap what we sow. It's a universal, timeless, natural law!

6. It's rough before you reap.

This harvest law will be a great source of encouragement to those about to give up on the brink of a miracle. Our investment and our risk are greatest just before harvest. After the farmer plants the seed, he must continue investing time and money into his crop, cultivating and fertilizing it. As the investment increases, so does the risk. If you have been planting and praying or maintaining, don't quit! Your crop could be just about to burst through the ground.

7. Perpetual planting equals repeated reaping.

Any farmer knows well that if he fed all of his grain to his livestock and didn't save any seed for the next spring's planting, he couldn't expect a crop. Similarly, if he didn't have the resources with which to buy seed, he couldn't very well hope to have a harvest that fall.

In most lives, consuming the entire harvest is the norm rather than exception, yet we wonder why we have no crop to harvest. We fail to plant by failing to take some of the love we receive and sowing it into the lives of those we meet. We eventually find ourselves without friends and living very lonely lives. We can reap a financial harvest by taking a portion of the money we earn and investing it into a worthy cause.

However, in most cases, we feel justified in not helping someone because of our own financial state of affairs. So we use our money to pay off the mortgage or car loan and, before we know it, there is no seed left to sow, money to give, time to contribute or love to share. It is important to consider the seed portion of any harvest as high priority and set it aside so it is available for planting when the season arrives or the opportunity arises. Don't eat your seeds.

I planted seeds right here. The plants should be 10 feet tall by now.

Go for it; start planting today. It's easy to know what seeds to plant, just determine what it is you want to reap. Remember the amount you reap is determined by the amount you sow! To reap a bountiful harvest, we must sow good seeds generously, in faith, believing that we will reap.

Somebody said it couldn't be done,
But with a chuckle he replied
That maybe it couldn't, but he would be one
Who wouldn't say no till he tried.
So he buckled right in with the trace of a grin
On his face. If he worried he hid it.
He started to sing as he tackled the thing
That couldn't be done and he did it.
Somebody scoffed "Oh, you'll never do that;
At least no one has ever done it."
But he took off his coat and he took off his hat
And the first thing he knew he had begun it.
With the lift of his chin and a bit of a grin,
Without any doubt or quiddit,
He started to sing as he tackled the thing
That couldn't be done and he did it.
There are thousands to tell you it cannot be done
There are thousands to prophesy failure;
There are thousands to point out to you, one by one.
The dangers that await to assail you
But just buckle right in with a bit of a grin,
Then take off your coat and go to it;
Just start in to sing as you tackle the thing
That "cannot be done" and you'll do it.

— Edgar A. Guest

CHAPTER — 13

*A*TTITUDE –
THE BIG DIFFERENCE

OUR ATTITUDE IS a combination of our thoughts, feelings and actions. Our attitude is our statement to the world of who we really are, regardless of what we say. Our life is merely a reflection of our attitudes.

"The environment you fashion out of your thoughts...your beliefs...your ideals...your philosophy is the only climate you will ever live in."—Alfred A. Montapert

Our attitude is the major factor in determining whether or not we will be successful in our careers and businesses, in the building of our families and in every other area of our lives. Positive thoughts are the seeds of positive attitudes, and positive attitudes are the seeds of positive results. A new attitude always produces a new result. The Bible says "You will be renewed by the renewing of your mind." To change who we are, we must change how we think. Prosperity definitely begins with a positive state of mind.

The thoughts we allow our mind to dwell on determine the way we feel, which ultimately is reflected in our actions. Unless we choose our own thoughts, we end up following the thoughts of others. Only we can master our own thoughts. *"What we think about, comes about. We are the products of our own thoughts."* Mark Victor Hansen says. We hold within ourselves everything that it takes to live a happy life. Happiness is not a destination but, rather, a way of traveling.

The elevation we can climb to in this life is determined solely by our attitude. Just like an airplane. When the attitude indicator indicates that the nose of the aircraft is pitched up, it means it is climbing and gaining altitude. What is your attitude indicator reading? Look up and you'll climb up.

A Harvard University study revealed that 85% of the reasons for success, accomplishments, promotions, etc. were a result of our attitudes and only 15% the result of technical expertise. Still, our present school system spends 90% of its education dollars on teaching facts, and only 10% on training our attitudes. Our mind is like a garden: it can give back only what we put into it.

"The mind is its own place, and in itself can make heaven of Hell, and hell of Heaven." - MILTON

FROM FAITH TO FEAR

I knew something was wrong in May 1987 when

thoughts of fear and unbelief began racing through my mind. I began to fear the worst for every area of my life. Every asset appeared as a potential liability. Every possible success loomed as a probable failure and every realizable gain looked like a possible loss. This was definitely my first experience with negativity and the fear of failure.

As I heard the prison doors of pessimism slam shut in my mind, my first fear was that I had been sentenced for life. Thank God, I found the keys to unlocking those gates, and I was once again able to experience the freedom of a positive mental attitude and faith. I chose to give myself my own reprieve. So can you! It is time to take control of your thoughts.

The Roman emperor Marcus Aurelius put it this way *"A man's life is what his thoughts make of it."*

"As a man thinketh in his heart, so is he." – The Bible

Thinking in your heart is different than thinking in your head. Thinking in your head is theology ... it's knowledge ... it's know-how. Thinking in your heart is what you really believe ... it's wisdom ... it's your passions ... your convictions ... your inner-drive.

THE OPTIMIST

There is a story of identical twins. One was a hope-filled optimist. *"Everything is coming up roses!"* he would say. The other was a sad and hopeless pessimist. He thought that Murphy, as in Murphy's Law, was an optimist. The worried parents of the boys brought them to the local psychologist.

He suggested to the parents a plan to balance the twins' personalities. *"On their next birthday, put them in separate rooms to open their gifts. Give the pessimist the best toys you can afford, and give the optimist a box of manure."* The parents followed these instructions and carefully observed the results.

When they peeked in on their pessimist, they heard him audibly complaining, *"I don't like the color of this computer....I'll bet this calculator will break....I don't like this game....I know someone who's got a bigger car than this...."*

Tiptoeing across the corridor, the parents peeked in and saw their little optimist gleefully throwing the manure up in the air. He was giggling. *"You can't fool me! Where there's this much manure, there's gotta be a pony!"*

– Author Unknown

from More Sower's Seeds *by* Brian Cavanaugh

The mind can only think one thought at a time, positive or negative. We and only we get to choose. In order to recover from burnout, I had to take control of my mind. I needed to stop thinking about the strange things I feared, and begin to have faith once again. I needed faith in God, and faith in myself.

Faith is what you have left after everything else has been lost. It is the ability to see the invisible.

"You are what you are and where you are because of what has gone into their mind. You can change what you are and where you are by changing what goes into your mind." — Zig Ziglar

ROTTEN THINKIN'
"Worry is a destructive process of occupying the mind with thoughts that are contrary to God's love and care"
Norman Vincent Peale

"Fear knocked on the door and faith opened it and lo, there was nothing there"- Bob Proctor. The fear of failure is the worst of all fears.

My dad was a dog breeder back home at the farm when I was growing up, and he would always tell us kids "A dog can tell if you are afraid." Well, I soon discovered that we can also transmit the destructive vibrations of fear to the minds of other human beings as well. As I became more fearful, I noticed the effect this had on the people around me. They quickly lost confidence in my ability to lead and make sound decisions.

BLA Vs. PMA

A positive mental attitude (PMA) will help you do anything you focus on, better than a negative mental attitude will. PMA will propel you faster in the direction you have chosen for your life but does not guarantee that you have the right road map or that you're headed in the right direction. Many positive people have achieved great things but lost their family, their health, and their soul in the process. PMA almost cost me all of the above, plus, it nearly cost me my life.

My discovery that PMA wasn't the complete answer to truly successful living came more like a revelation during my horrific burnout experience. The alternative I found, which I call "A Balanced Life Attitude (BLA)," will take you from mediocrity to excellence in every area of your life, not only those areas you consider important to you at the present time.

YOU CAN BE POSITIVE WITHOUT BEING BALANCED, BUT YOU CAN'T BE BALANCED WITHOUT BEING POSITIVE.

A positive mental attitude is the first step to achieving a balanced life attitude but can't be considered a substitute for the real thing.

A Balanced Life Attitude is the secret to:
- Peak performance without burnout
- Being spiritual without necessarily being religious
- Being wealthy without being greedy
- Being confident without being arrogant
- Believing in yourself without losing faith in God
- Being positive and not humanistic
- Being powerful without being proud
- Realism without negativity
- Humility without losing your self-esteem

HAPPY HOUR —
THE PRELUDE TO A WONDERFUL DAY

The early morning hours set the stage for your entire day. Most people sleep a half an hour too long every day. Sleeping as late as possible, they gulp down a cup of coffee while dodging traffic and cussing at the guy who just cut them off. That does not make for starting your day in a frame of mind that is happy, peaceful, positive and powerful. Before my burnout experience, that was how I started every day.

In Sept. 1987 as I was recovering from burnout, I made a commitment to dedicate the first hour of every day to meditation, singing, prayer, goal-setting, reading and physical exercise in solitude. This has since become a high priority in my life. I'm positive because I decided to be positive when I got out of bed this morning.

EARLY TO RISE

The first thing I had to do was to form the habit of early rising. I had never been an early riser; my mom called me a night owl. What better time of the day to get yourself in tune with the God that controls the universe than early in the morning, when all is quiet and our mind is alert and fresh?

"To do much clear thinking, a man must arrange regular periods when he can concentrate and indulge his imagination without distraction." – Thomas A. Edison

During my happy hour, *I kill two stones with one bird,* by combining my exercise with my thinking and prayer time, I work on 2 goals at the same time. Jogging and swimming are my favorite forms of exercise. Since I live on a thirteen-acre hobby farm, a jog in the country is just outside the front door, and with an indoor pool, we swim all year around.

PRAYER

I begin my prayer time by giving thanks for all the good things in my life.

- A beautiful spouse, who loves and cares for me.
- Four wonderful kids.
- My mom, dad, brothers and sisters.
- A creative mind and healthy body.
- My Creator, who supplies all my needs.
- An abundantly happy and successful life.
- The prosperous businesses and projects in which I am involved.
- My church and friends.

Secondly, I forgive all the people in my life who may have transgressed against me at any time, in any way, for any reason. I then confess to God my shortcomings and thank him for His forgiveness and the clean slate with which I can now begin my day. Next, I turn my thoughts to my own personal needs, challenges and opportunities, believing that God wants the best for my life and that I'll receive what I ask for, I ask in detail. I ask for Divine wisdom to fill my being, so that I may be ready at all times to make wise, intelligent and timely decisions.

"Wisdom entereth not into a malicious mind."

– Rabelais

Wisdom is my number one prayer request, because I believe to have God's wisdom is to hold the keys to the abundant life He desires us to live. I then ask Him to meet any financial, physical or other needs that I may have.

Finally, my daily prayer is that I may be a blessing to everyone I meet and that my cup will be full and running over. I pray that I will prosper in all my ways, and that I will be blest, so that I can be a blessing to others. I then thank God again for all the wonderful things He means to me and for the personal relationship I can have with my Creator.

To conclude my power hour, I take a warm shower. While the warm water flows over my body, I sing and think happy, positive thoughts. I simply let the water wash away any negative thoughts or tiredness from my body.

Before I leave for work, I spend ten to fifteen minutes with my wife, praying and reading the Bible together. The Book of Proverbs contains a vast amount of practical wisdom for operating a business and also contains many successful living principles. We conclude our time together with prayer, asking God's blessing on each other for the day, before we part. The support of those we love is so vital to our success as human beings that, without it, we would never reach full potential in any area of our lives.

The following quotation is one that I believe should be hanging on all bathroom mirrors around the world:

I got up early one morning
And rushed right into the day.
I had so much to accomplish
That I didn't have time to pray.
Problems just tumbled about me and
heavier came each task.
"Why doesn't God help me?" I wondered,
He answered, "You didn't ask."
I wanted to see joy and beauty,
But the day toiled on grey and bleak,
I wondered why God didn't show me,
He said, "But you didn't seek."
I tried to come into God's presence,

I tried all the keys at the lock,
God gently and lovingly chided,
"My child, you didn't knock."
I woke up early this morning,
And paused before entering the day.
I had so much to accomplish,
That I had to take time to pray.

The Optimist Club has adopted a creed, called *"My Attitude,"* a prayer or affirmation that will virtually change your life if you've been living with a negative attitude.

- To be so strong that nothing can disturb my peace of mind.
- To talk health, happiness and prosperity to every person I meet.
- To make all my friends feel there is something in them.
- To look at the sunny side of everything and make my optimism come true.
- To think only the best, to work only for the best, and expect only the best.
- To be just as enthusiastic about the success of others as I am of my own.
- To forget the mistakes of the past and press on to the greater achievements of the future.
- To wear a cheery countenance at all times and give every living creature I meet a smile.
- To give so much time to the improvement of myself, that I have no time to critisize others.
- To be too large for worry, too noble for anger, too strong for fear, and too happy to permit the pressure of trouble.

LEARNING TIME

Peter Drucker says, *"Knowledge has to be improved, challenged and increased constantly, or it vanishes."*

The drive to and from work is an excellent time to listen to motivational and inspirational tapes. Cavett Robert says, *"Make your driving time learning time. Get a classroom on wheels."* That's what I have. The average person can get the equivalent of two university courses a year just sitting behind a windshield going to and from work.

Attending inspirational and educational seminars has also proven to be a wise investment into my mind. The best return of any investment is the investment into your own mind, usually a 100% return or more the first year.

"Five years from now, you will be the same person you are today except for the people you meet, the books you read, and the tapes you hear." — Charles "Tremendous" Jones

Not all readers are leaders, but all leaders are readers. My library is filled with good books that have inspired, motivated and empowered me to achieve my goals. My goal is to read one book every two weeks. I read books that are inspirational and educational.

NO PROBLEMS ONLY CHALLENGES

"Problem" is one of the words I have chosen to remove from my vocabulary. I have replaced it with the word *"challenge."* I even forbid my family or employees to come to me with the statement — *"we have a problem."* Their perception of the situation as a problem does not change my perception of it as an opportunity for growth or a challenge. Often *opportunities* come disguised as *problems.*

Doctor Norman Vincent Peale tells the story of a young man coming up to him on fifth avenue in New York City, grabbing him by the lapels and saying, *"Doctor Peale, please help me. I can't handle my problems. They are just too much."*

Doctor Peale said, *"Look, I have got to give a talk. If you will let go of my lapels, I will show you a place where there are people with no problems."*

The man said, *"If you can do that, I would give anything to go there."*

Doctor Peale said, *"You may not want to go there, once you see the place. It is two blocks away."*

They walked up to the Forest Lawn Cemetery and Doctor Peale said, *"Look, there are one hundred and fifty thousand people in there. I happen to know that none of them have a problem."*

Most people, unless suicidal, would not consider joining the ranks of the deceased in Forest Lawn Cemetery, a drastic move just to escape their problems. However, in reality, they have never really "lived." Their attitudes have caused them to lead a morbid existence they think is called life.

An eagle is an excellent example of how to face the storms that blow into our lives from time to time. The eagle, long a symbol of freedom and power, can sense the storm coming and begins to fly right into its eye. The eagle sets its wings to catch the air currents, which carry it to an altitude above the storm, where it simply waits the storm out.

We too can meet challenges in our lives head on and soar above them like an eagle. We can experience that same freedom and power, or we can spend our lives as a turkey on the ground letting the storms of life beat down on us as we complain about our problems. Are you a turkey or an eagle? You choose. Your attitude will determine your altitude just as it does for an eagle. Choose a positive mental attitude and then soar with the eagles.

LETTING IT RUB OFF

A positive mental attitude empowers, encourages and enriches those around us as we radiate forth an aura of peace, love, joy and self confidence without arrogance.

In North America, at the time of writing this book, we are just beginning to recover from a five-year economic recession that has been the worst since the great depression of the 1930s. However, it was only a recession for those who chose to participate in it with their attitudes. Personally, I chose not to, and that fact became obvious to the people I was doing business with. My attitude said, "This is not a recession but a fantastic opportunity for growth and market share."

Several years ago, I received a phone call from our Account Manager at a major chartered bank that does some of our project financing. The call began with the usual *"Hi! How is business?"* When I responded "Great!" She explained, *"Gee Ben, I don't know what it is you have got, but you should bottle it and start selling it."* The best part is, it is free. A positive attitude is yours for the choosing.

Surround yourself with the most positive people you can find. Negative people will pull you down more quickly than you can pull them up. Avoid negative people with all your power. Negativity is contagious. Don't live in the negative, when you believe in the positive.

Two frogs fell into a can of cream

- or so I've heard it told.

The sides of the can were shinny and steep,

The cream was deep and cold.

"Oh, what's the use?" said no. 1,

" 'tis fate — no help is around —

Good-bye, my friend! Good-bye, sad world!"

And weeping still he drowned.

But no. 2 of sterner stuff,

dog-paddled in surprise,

The while he wiped his creamy face

and wiped his creamy eyes.

"I'll swim awhile at least," he said

- or so it has been said —

"It wouldn't really help the world

if one more frog was dead."

An hour or two he kicked and swam

not once he stopped to mutter,

But kicked and swam, and swam and kicked,

then hopped out, via butter.

- Author Unknown —

CHAPTER — 14

THE POWER OF WEALTH –

Most people believe that, if they earned more money, they would be happy. They think that, with a bigger income, their problems will disappear. I can tell you from experience that it's more fun earning a half million dollars a year than losing a half million dollars a year. I've done both! However, the true joy didn't come from just making the money, but also from sharing it with others. The power of money is truly amazing. If placed in the right hands it can help, heal and create value for yourself and others.

CREATING WEALTH

The first key to mastering your financial life is the ability to create wealth. Notice, I didn't say earn wealth.

True wealth cannot be earned, it must be created. We are all rewarded in direct proportion to our contribution to society. If we increase the value of what we contribute our income will increase accordingly.

I can hear you asking "Well then, what about Mother Theresa? Look at her value to society, and she's not rich." Perhaps then, you still don't understand the Laws Of The Harvest. Mother Theresa plants love, not money; that's why she is the most-loved person in the world. Who wouldn't love a person like her?

Start by asking yourself, "How can I achieve what I'm doing in less time? In what ways can I reduce production costs? What career change would increase the value of my time?" Earning more doesn't necessarily mean working longer hours.

MAINTAINING YOUR WEALTH

The key to hanging on to your wealth, needless to say, is spending less than you earn. Sounds easy, but it's amazing how fast your spending catches up to your earning and quickly outpaces it if left unchecked.

MULTIPLYING YOUR WEALTH

Multiplication of wealth comes from investing your money and the magic of *compound interest*. Compound interest means that your interest starts to earn you more interest.

The other way to rapidly grow your wealth is called *leverage.* A lot riskier, but a whole lot more fun! A good example of leverage is to purchase a piece of real-estate for $100,000 with a 10% down payment. Suppose you sold that property in a year for $10,000 profit. That would be a 10% profit but, it would be a 100% return on investment.

PROTECTION OF YOUR WEALTH

In today's litigious society, asset protection is a very important subject. The wealthy have their heads above the crowd and are the ones susceptible to lawsuits, many of which are frivolous. The best advice here is to consult an expert before you need to.

There are, however, two assets that I have found to be not only valuable, but totally creditor-proof; what you gain by experience and what you give away with no strings attached. So you see, there is no way you can lose everything.

ENJOYING YOUR WEALTH

Too many people wait for retirement to enjoy their wealth. Unfortunately, many never make it to that stage of life.

Start right now to enjoy your wealth by rewarding yourself on occasion for a job well done. Begin now to celebrate your victories.

Nothing gives more enjoyment than sharing your wealth. Anthony Robbins says, *"True wealth is an emotion, a sense of absolute abundance."*

SHARING YOUR WEALTH

The law of giving is another universal success principle that operates whether we believe in it or not. I have personally been applying the principles of giving money, time and love in my business and personal life for the past ten years. It works! My wife and I have experienced the miracle of giving as we have given virtually hundreds of thousands of dollars and have watched it return in abundance. It is sometimes like trying to take a drink from a fire hydrant. It is hard to take it all in.

The Bible says in Luke 6:38, *"Give and it shall be given unto you: good measure pressed down and shaken together, and running over, shall men give into your bosom. For with the same measure that you measure withal, it shall be measured to you again."*

So I give expecting to receive. That is what the Law says, and that is how it works. Giving with the expectation to receive something in return is not wrong or selfish if our motives are right and we continue to use our resources to bless others.

I deeply admire and respect the great business men such as Paul J. Meyer and R.G. LeTrourneau, who generously shared their vast wealth with others. They also attributed much of their success to the Law of Giving. I am also thankful that they were willing to leave behind a challenge for businessmen like me, by sharing their experiences in writing. There are many other businesses and individuals today, besides me, who are experiencing the miracle of giving, in good times and bad. Why? Because the "law of giving" knows nothing of this thing we call recession.

McDonald's Restaurants is involved in giving in a big way. Their Ronald McDonald Houses provide shelter to parents while their children are hospitalized. This company has experienced tremendous growth in a shrinking market and a seven hundred million dollar profit in 1991, when many companies and franchises were closing their doors.

Stanley Tam (U.S. Plastics) got started with giving when he first started his business and did not have enough money to put gas in his car, as a salesman on the road. Today, he gives away close to two million dollars a year. He says, *"I shovel it out and God keeps shoveling it back in and He has a bigger shovel."*

Rich DeVos of Amway donated one million dollars to Robert Schuller to help build the Crystal Cathedral. In 1991, the Amway Corporation grew to 3.1 billion dollars in sales from 2 billion the year before, the largest growth in corporate history.

Paul J. Meyers, the founder of Success Motivation Institute Inc., is another truly remarkable individual who owns more than 40 businesses and gives 50% of his income to charities. His donations average $342,000 a month.

GIVE YOUR FIRST FRUITS, NOT YOUR LEFTOVERS.

If you want the best, give the best. Too many people only give away their garbage and wonder why that's all they get out of life.

I have heard Bob Proctor say, *"We are all born rich; it is just that some of us are short of cash."* The favorite excuse for people not to give is that they "can't afford to" or they are "short of cash." Let me tell you from experience, you can't afford not to. Let's be honest; we can afford anything within reason if it's a priority and we want it badly enough. Unless giving becomes a priority, there will never be enough time or money left to give. Give your best, not your leftovers.

So often I hear people say, "I'll start giving after all my debts are paid-off." That's like saying "I'll start to plant after I harvest my first crop." The Law of Giving only works one way: "give and it shall be given unto you." Nowhere will you ever find this law operating in reverse. We must always give or plant first. We must also always plant or give whatever it is we expect to harvest or receive in return.

WHERE, OR TO WHOM DO I GIVE?

Can you imagine someone eating their lunch at McDonald's and paying for it at Burger King? That sounds absurd, but that's what many people do with their giving.

I believe your tithe, or ten percent of your income, belongs to the ministry that feeds you spiritually. I know some of you are asking, is that ten percent before or after taxes? If that is the case, you have obviously missed the point of first fruit giving. The balance of your giving should go to worthwhile charitable organizations that are financially responsible and accountable, or wherever you see a need. Listen to your heart. It'll tell you what to do.

HOW DO I GIVE?

Giving must be joyfully done for it to be effective. Nothing in the world is more satisfying or more fun than giving, if your attitude is right. I hate to receive a gift if I know the giver is reluctant to give it. We all love a cheerful giver, and so does God.

Plan your giving by placing into your personal budget, at the beginning of each year, an item called charitable donations. Budget your giving right after your income and just before your taxes. Last-minute panic giving can often take place with a grudging attitude. Plan your giving and become a joyful giver. *"Abundant living requires abundant giving"*

RISK

When most people think of assets, they think of money or a column of their financial statements representing the things they own. However, our assets also include things such as our time, our talents, our potential, our health, our creative abilities, our faith, our family, our friends, and so on.

Ownership of an asset simply means we have title to it. It does not mean that we manage, enjoy or take advantage of the fact that we are in possession of it, nor does it mean that we share these assets with the people around us. Ownership means just that, "We own it."

USE THEM OR LOSE THEM

When it comes to our skills and talents, we often neglect to use the full potential that God has given us. That potential may allow us to accomplish great things in our chosen vocation, yet often we choose the life of mediocrity instead of excellence. Treat your skills and abilities as your greatest assets. Put each asset to its highest and best use. Only then can you realize their full value.

TIME

Time is the greatest asset any person can own, yet it is the only asset given equally to all people at birth. What we accomplish in the twenty-four hours a day given us is determined by the way we manage our time or, more accurately, ourselves. Managing our time properly will greatly reduce the amount of stress we experience in our lives. Stress is normally caused by working under pressure towards a deadline, which is the main reason people fail to set, or choose not to set, goals for their lives.

Make a *To Do List* at the end of each day for the following day. Determine the priority of each item on your list. Prioritize. Do not let others steal your time. It is the most valuable asset you have. How you utilize your time will determine how time uses you.

Share your assets. Do not hoard them. Sharing your assets is the best way to avoid a greedy, selfish attitude. The sharing of what you own makes ownership so much more fun. Giving people rides in my helicopter, watching people ride our horses, drive my ATV, ride my snowmobile, or swim in our pool gives me as much pleasure as enjoying them myself. There goes the Law Of Giving again.

RISK THEM DON'T BURY THEM

Most people won't step out of the boat, yet they expect to walk on the water. Most people tiptoe through life, playing it safe, hoping to arrive at retirement, arriving only to find they now regret the fact that they never dared to venture outside their comfort zone. They feel they have wasted so much of their potential. Then again, they will never really know what their potential was, because they never dared to win. They never stepped out in faith because of the fear they may sink. Instead, they sat in the boat until it sank. That is existence, not living! There is a difference.

We either step forward into fear or back into safety. We were born to win, but conditioned to lose. We let other people put a lid on our potential. Get out of the boat, step onto the water and watch the miracles happen in your life. Go for it!!!

All things are possible for those who believe. So instead of saying I'll believe it when I see it, start believing. You will see it.

Risks must be taken, because the greatest hazard in life is to risk nothing. The person who risks nothing, does nothing, has nothing and is nothing. There is no success or failure without risk!

You may avoid suffering and sorrow, but simply cannot learn, feel, change, grow, love and live. Chained by the certitudes, you are a slave who has forfeited freedom. You are only free if you take risks!

RISKS

To laugh is to risk appearing the fool

To weep is to risk appearing sentimental

To reach out for another is to risk involvement

To expose feelings is to risk exposing your true self

To place your ideas, your dreams before the crowd is to

risk their loss

To love is to risk not being loved In return

To live is to risk dying

To hope is to risk despair

To try is to risk failure

CHAPTER — 15

INTEGRITY, HONESTY & CHARACTER

Habits are like a cable that we weave every day. Before long those tiny strands are woven into a cable that is difficult to break.

"Thoughts lead on to purpose; purposes go forth in action; actions form habits; habits decide character; and character fixes our destiny." - TYRON EDWARDS

The force of habit can quickly push us to success or failure. The more often we do something, the more likely we are to do it again. Habit can be the best servant or the worst master. What we first choose, in the end becomes a compulsion. Habits, good or bad, always bring some sort of satisfaction. We can only get rid of our habits by seeking another, better form of satisfying those needs.

HABITS

I am your constant companion.
I am your greatest helper or your heaviest burden.
I will push you onward or drag you down to failure.
I am completely at your command.
Half the things you do, you might just as well turn over to me,
And I will be able to do as quickly and as correctly.
I am easily managed; you must be merely firm with me.
Show me exactly how you want something done,
After a few lessons, I will do it automatically.
I am the servant of all great men.
And, alas, of all failures as well.
Those who are great, I have made great.
Those who are failures, I have made failures.
I am not a machine, though I work with all the precision of a machine.
Plus the intelligence of a man.
You may run me for profit or run me for ruin;
It makes no difference to me.
Take me, train me, be firm with me
And I will put the world at your feet.
Be easy with me, and I will destroy you.
Who am I?
I am HABIT!

– AUTHOR UNKNOWN

CHARACTER

Character is the ability to carry out a worthy decision after the emotion of making it has worn off. These seven traits are common to people with good character:

1. **Goodness** Being good, doesn't mean being goody-goody. Some people are so sanctimonious they turn everyone off — including God sometimes. You

know the self-righteous king I'm talking about. I've heard it said that "the difference between a Christian and a politician is that: "politicians confess each others sins, Christians confess their own." Goodness is not being intolerant of the sins of others, but rather, being intolerant of our own.

Goodness does not come with religion and, likewise, goodness does not automatically come with compassion. Goodness must be added to faith, and compassion must be added to goodness. What a pity to see a good person who has no compassion for hungry or hurting or lonely people. What a waste!

2. **Knowledge** The ignorant fail because they won't study or search or think, and some even take a perverse pride in being ignorant, as if they were better because of it. However, many educated people fail because they lack wisdom. Wisdom is: "the skillful application of knowledge." The educated have the information, the wise know how to apply it.

The first step to freedom is knowing the truth. Next, we need self-control to act on the truth we now know.

3. **Self-control** Self-control is the power to do what you want to do. Self-control is more critical to a person's true, lasting success than natural power or talent.

An athlete must embrace a rigorous training discipline in order to be competitive. Most people fail to reach their full potential in achieving true success and happiness because they are like the born-athlete who lacks the self-control to train. Instead of experiencing victory and receiving the gold medal, they live their lives in mediocrity, satisfied to say, that they ran the race. We can never reach our full potential in life without self-control.

Without self-control, we are heading down a road to self-destruction. Like a vehicle out of control, people that lack self-control have little idea where they will end up or what damage will occur in the process. Self-control keeps us headed in the right direction, provided we have chosen the right road to follow. When we are in control, we change direction at will.

Changing our destination requires time. Even though we may be in control and able to change direction immediately, change in destination requires the time to travel towards it. True freedom in life comes from doing what you, the inner person, would like to do, rather than being simply driven by external forces and the passions of our humanity.

Self-control is the ability to discipline ones self. Stephen R. Covey, the author of *The Seven Habits of Highly Effective People*, defines discipline as "the ability to make and keep promises".

4. Godliness It's strange, the way we think about godliness. We are hesitant to claim we have it, yet are insulted if we are called ungodly. Godliness means "to be well devout" or as Micah puts it "to walk humbly with God."

Godliness requires several elements:

- The recognition that there is a God, one that has created and now sustains us.

- An awareness of His presence in your life. He is right here, right now!

- A devotion to Him. Be ready to do God's will.

5. Kindness A people-loving attitude, that's what kindness is. Kindness reaches out to a broken heart and offers a healing touch, a hug, when it seems no one cares or understands. Hurting people are just aching for someone to reach out and put their arms around them. You have my permission to hug first and ask questions later. Yes, there are those individuals that will resist your gesture of a hug; many of them may have been victims of abuse in their past. Hug them anyway.

Kindness is reaching out to help an elderly person. I never forget walking my grandpa home from church every Sunday. Holding his cane in one hand and my arm in the other, he would walk with me arm in arm. I would sit and talk to Grandpa for hours. He had all the time in the world for me. He treated me as an equal, as an adult. He was so kind to me.

Kindness means helping the poor when you'd just rather look the other way. It's an attitude of compassion that reaches out to pick up and never puts down.

Kindness is taking time to reach out to the sick. I can't help but think about Mark Victor Hansen and the touching story he tells about Bopsy.

The 26-year-old mother stared down at her son, who was dying of terminal leukemia. Although her heart was filled with sadness, she also had a strong feeling of determination. Like any parent, she wanted her son to grow up and fulfill all his dreams. Now that was no longer possible. The leukemia would see to that. But she still wanted her sons dreams to come true.

She took her son's hand and asked, "Bopsy, did you ever think about what you wanted to be when you grew up? Did you ever dream about what you wanted to do with your life?"

"Mommy, I always wanted to be a fireman when I grew up."

Mom smiled back and said, "Let's see if we can

make your wish come true." Later that day, she went to her local fire department in Phoenix, Arizona, where she met Fireman Bob, who had a heart as big as Phoenix. She explained her son's final wish and asked if it might be possible to give her six-year-old son a ride around the block on a fire engine.

Fireman Bob said, "Look, we can do better than that. If you'll have your son ready at seven o'clock Wednesday morning, we'll make him an honorary fire-man for the whole day. He can come down to the fire station and eat with us, go out on all the fire calls, the whole nine yards! And, if you'll give us his sizes, we'll get a real fire uniform made for him, with a real fire hat - not a toy one - with the emblem of the Phoenix Fire Department on it, a yellow slicker like we wear and rubber boots. They are all manufactured right here in Phoenix, so we can get them fast."

Three days later, Fireman Bob picked up Bopsy, dressed him in fire uniform and escorted him from his hospital to the waiting hook and ladder truck. Bopsy got to sit up on the back of the truck and help steer it back to the station. He was in heaven.

There were three fire calls in Phoenix that day and Bopsy got to go out on all three calls. He rode in the different fire engines, the paramedic's van and even the fire chief's car. He was also videotaped for the local news program.

Having all his dreams come true, with all the love and attention lavished upon him, so deeply touched Bopsy that he lived three months longer than any doctor thought possible.

One night all of his vital signs dropped dramatically and the head nurse, who believed in the Hospice concept that no one should die alone, began to call the family members to the hospital. Then she remembered the day Bopsy had spent as a fireman, so she called the fire chief and asked if it would be possible to send a fireman in uniform to the hospital to be with Bopsy as he made his transition. The chief replied, "We can do better than that. We'll be there in five minutes. Will you please do me a favor? When you hear the sirens screaming and see the lights flashing, will you announce over the PA system that there is not a fire? It's just the fire department coming to see one of its finest members one more time. And will you open the window to his room? Thanks."

About five minutes later a hook and ladder truck arrived at the hospital, extended its ladder up to Bopsy's third floor open window and 14 fireman and two firewomen climbed up the ladder into Bopsy's room. With his mother's permission, they hugged him and held him and told him how much they loved him.

With his dying breath, Bopsy looked up at the fire chief and said, "Chief am I really a fireman now?"

"Bopsy, you are," the fire chief said. With those words, Bopsy smiled and closed his eyes for the last time.

– Jack Canfield and Mark Victor Hansen

6. **Love**   Love is probably the most important ingredient of success. Without it, our lives echo hollow and empty. With it, our lives have meaning and warmth. We can only learn to live, if we learn to love.

7. **Perseverance**   *"If I had to select one quality: one personal characteristic that I regard as being most highly correlated with success, whatever the field, I would pick persistence. Determination. The will to endure to the end, to get knocked down seventy times and get off the floor saying, Here goes number*

seventy-one!"

– RICHARD M. DeVOS

Abraham Lincoln, one of the greatest presidents of America, failed six times in trying for political office. He also won six times and eventually became President.

Thomas Edison, the great inventor best known for the creation of the light bulb, conducted some 18,000 experiments before reaching his goal. Some people would say he failed 18,000 times.

Has your past been filled with failures or experiments? It is much easier to persevere if you look at them as experiments.

"Most people give up just when they are about to achieve success. They quit on the one yard line. They give up at the last minute of the game, one foot from a winning touchdown."

- H. ROSS PEROT

Perseverance requires patience, a virtue rarely found in highly-motivated, high-energy people like me. Since it doesn't come naturally to us, we need to make it a learned skill. Our kids are sometimes our best teachers of patience.

DRIFTING

The most common reason for the lack of persistence is the drift. How do we motivate ourselves to keep going? Here is the secret. We simply remind ourselves of why we began. Most of us have experienced this drift principle in the area of exercise. We hear someone say how good jogging is for our health. We faithfully begin jogging every morning. Before we know it, it's once a month. We set out on the right course, yet somehow we seem to be nudged off course along the way by an unseen elbow in our side.

SELF-PITY

The "poor me" attitude is not one that produces endurance. A lot of people settle for a *pity party* whereas, if they just kept going a little bit longer, they could be celebrating with a *victory* party.

CHAPTER — 16

THE JOY OF HUGGING

FROM CHILDHOOD ON, we are all in need of love in order to live a balanced life. Our need for love does not diminish with age, but actually becomes a key ingredient to a healthy self-esteem as we become adults. Without it, our life is hollow and echoes with emptiness. With it, our life vibrates with warmth and meaning. Love makes the difference between living and breathing. Only when we learn to love, can we learn to live.

"You will find when you look back on life that the moments when you have really lived, are the moments when you have done things in a spirit of love."

– Henry Drummond

A healthy, balanced, successful person can be totally crushed by the withdrawal of love. Many financially successful businesspeople and executives that are peak performers take their spouses' love for granted. They feel that the supporting love of their spouse at home, giving them the self-confidence and self-esteem they need to be super-achievers, not realizing that their wives want love in return. When they discover that their spouses are leaving them, they are stunned. Many go into a state of depression, lose their appetite, cannot concentrate, have difficulty sleeping, and perform poorly in their job. Some even commit suicide.

On more than one occasion have I had to convince a successful businessman that suicide was not the solution just because his wife had left him.

Many times, a spouse will withhold love to express displeasure with something a partner has said or done simply because this punishment has proved to be very effective. Sometimes this withholding of love is involuntary, perhaps a part of man's emotional cycle. Or it can simply be a symptom of hormonal changes during a woman's monthly cycle, known as pre-menstrual syndrome, or PMS. PMS can cause a normally happy loving wife to become depressed, irritable and orally abusive toward her husband in the seven to ten days before the menstrual period. The good news is that PMS symptoms are found in only ten percent of women and they cease at menopause.

If you are in this situation, it is helpful to understand the changes in your wife's behavior. Your self-esteem will not suffer when you realize that she may not be in control of her feelings at certain times of the month.

As we experience the love of people, we feel a sense of

worth in ourselves. Love affects our performance at work, our ability to think, and the way we handle stress. We perceive our own value based on the amount of love we receive. We all need daily reassurance that we are loved.

Every chance to give love is an opportunity to receive it. The universal law of giving applies here again. The more you give love away, the more love comes back to you. Love others and they will love you.

HUGGING

I am into hugging. I have been known to hug anyone in sight at times, which can be embarrassing for the macho guy who can't even remember his own father taking him into his arms and hugging him. I seize every opportunity to give a hug and have set a goal to give at least twelve hugs a day. It is great, because giving a hug usually means receiving a hug in return.

With a wife and four children, I sometimes get my quota before leaving the house in the morning. Try a hug and a kiss with a cheery "good morning," another hug and a kiss when you leave for work and the same when you arrive home from work. Give them the final hug and a kiss when you have tucked them in and told them their bedtime stories. The last thing they experience before closing their little eyes is the love of their parents, and this love is the first thing to greet them in the morning.

Every morning when he arrives at the office, I give my brother a big hug and often we will say "I love you" to each other. Hugs are a wonderful way to start the day.

Mark and Patty Hanson conducted a *National Hug Survey* and discovered that 83% of the people surveyed grew up receiving less than one hug a day. Hugging is a beautiful way of giving and instantly receiving love from another person.

Hugging is universal. I have hugged people in many different countries of the world and, several years ago, my wife and I had the opportunity to share hugs with many little orphans in Guatemala. As we visited the feeding centers, the orphanages and even the city dump, we found children starving for something more than food. It was love.

I'll never forget my first visit to a feeding center located in the squatter's village of Mesquital on the south side of Guatemala City. These people had fled from the mountains to escape the rebel army and to seek a new life in the city. However, when they arrived, they discovered that there were no jobs and no affordable housing.

Each family simply started to construct a home with what ever scrap materials could be salvaged from the local dump. Most homes are constructed of odd shapes of cardboard, tin and scrap lumber of every dimension. There is no space between each home. Each house is just build against another. The average size of these homes is approximately 200 square feet with no electricity or running water.

Imagine with me, the site: No paved streets - just a dirt path the width of a vehicle. No sidewalks - just open sewers running along the side of the road. No windows or doors - just old sheets hanging over the openings. No grass or landscaped areas for the kids to play on - just mud and dirt. No side streets - only an alley wide enough for a foot path and, you guessed it - an open sewer.

As our vehicle pulled into this "Hell-hole" and I witnessed the site I just described and as the sickening smell of people burning whatever they could find to burn as cooking fuel reached my nostrils, I began to cry. This experience caused my life to change forever. Five years later, as I share with you this experience, the tears come again.

My first thought as I stepped out of that vehicle was "O Lord, forgive me when I whine." I made a commitment right then and there, to myself and my Creator, that I would do my part in making the world a better place, that I would be bold enough to make a difference.

The next site literally tore my heart out. Kids came running from everywhere, yelling "Gringos." The Americans who had started this feeding program which consisted of a Bible lesson and a warm meal twice a week, were affectionately referred to by these kids as "Gringos." What took me by surprise was the fact that these kids were not afraid of me, a perfect stranger to them. As I knelt down and stretched out my arms and began hugging those dirty little kids, I made the startling realization that these kids were starving for more than food; they were starving for affection and love.

One little four-year old boy just wouldn't let go of me. He wrapped his arms around my neck and pressed his cheek against mine. I carried him that way as I followed the rest of the kids down a narrow path between two rows of shacks to the one used as the feeding center. I stooped to avoid hitting my head in the doorway as I entered a dimly lit room filled with rows of narrow benches. As the program began that afternoon with the kids singing at the top of their lungs, my little friend relaxed his grip around my neck and fell asleep on my lap. What a picture! As if to say, "I've finally found a friend who will love me and who cares about me."

After their Bible lesson each child was served a portion

of black beans and bread. Of course, I had to sit beside my little friend and feed him.

It was difficult leaving those kids that day. However, I did depart a changed person, and I did leave a little piece of my heart there that day.

I've hugged dozens of kids with Aids while visiting a hospital for children with the disease in Constanta, Romania. I've hugged the street kids in Brazil, some as young as five years old, without parents and living on the street. I've picked up those little children as they reached out for love and have given them a hug. Each time my eyes have filled with tears as I acquired a new appreciation for the thing called *love.*

MISSIONARY VENTURES

Determined to do our part in sharing our love with the rest of the world, we have founded an organization called *Missionary Ventures of Canada*, a non-denominational mission that meets human needs through personal involvement. We send medical, dental and construction teams to third world countries sharing God's love and His Word. Our focus has been the construction of schools in Guatemala. As a result of my first visit to that country and the vision it inspired, thousands of children attend schools built by Canadians who volunteered their time and gave their money.

A recent newspaper article warned school teachers to refrain from hugging pupils since teachers are becoming targets of sexual abuse accusations. How tragic that our society considers taboo the practice of hugging (which is really a non-sexual expression of love) between teacher and pupil, between ourselves and people we have just met, and between one man and another.

THE HUGGING JUDGE

Lee Shapiro is a retired judge. At one point in his career, Lee realized that love is the greatest power there is. As a result, Lee became a hugger. He began offering everyone hugs. His colleagues dubbed him "the hugging judge"(as opposed to hanging judge, I suppose). The bumper sticker on his car reads, "Don't bug me! Hug me!"

About six years ago, Lee created what he calls his Hugger Kit. On the outside it reads, "A heart for a hug." The inside contains thirty little red embroidered hearts with stickums on the back. Lee will take out his Hugger Kit, go around to people and offer them a little red heart in exchange for a hug.

Lee has become so well known for this that he is often invited to keynote conferences and conventions, where he shares his message of unconditional love. At a conference in San Francisco, the local news media challenged him by saying, "It is easy to give out hugs here in the conference to people who self-selected to be here. But this would never work in the real world"

They challenged Lee to give away some hugs on the streets of San Francisco. Followed by a television crew from the local news station, Lee went out onto the street. First he approached a woman walking by. "Hi, I'm Lee Shapiro, the hugging judge. I'm giving out these hearts in exchange for a hug." "Sure," she replied. "Too easy," challenged the local commentator. Lee looked around. He saw a meter maid who was being given a hard time by the owner of a BMW to whom she was giving a ticket. He marched up to her, camera crew in tow, and said, "You look like you could use a hug. I'm the hugging judge and I'm offering you one." She accepted.

The television commentator threw down one final

challenge. "Look, here comes a bus. San Francisco bus drivers are the toughest, crabbiest, meanest people in the whole town. Let's see you get him to hug you." Lee took the challenge.

As the bus pulled up to the curb, Lee said, "Hi, I'm Lee Shapiro, the hugging judge. This has got to be one of the most stressful jobs in the whole world. I'm offering hugs to people today to lighten the load a little. Would you like one?" The six-foot-two, 230-pound bus driver got out of his seat, stepped down and said, "Why not?"

Lee hugged him, gave him a heart and waved good-bye as the bus pulled out. The TV crew was speechless. Finally, the commentator said, "I have to admit, I'm very impressed."

One day Lee's friend Nancy Johnston showed up on his doorstep. Nancy is a professional clown and she was wearing her clown costume, makeup and all. "Lee, grab a bunch of your Hugger Kits and let's go out to the home for the disabled."

When they arrived at the home, they started giving out balloon hats, hearts and hugs to the patients. Lee was uncomfortable. He had never before hugged people who were terminally ill, severely retarded or quadriplegic. It was definitely a stretch. But after a while it became easier with Nancy and Lee acquiring an entourage of doctors, nurses and orderlies who followed them from ward to ward.

After several hours, they reached the last ward. These were 34 of the worst cases Lee had seen in his life. The feeling was so grim it took his heart away. But out of their commitment to share their love and to make a difference, Nancy and Lee started working their way around the room followed by the medical staff, all of whom by now had hearts on their collars and balloon hats on their heads.

Finally, Lee came to the last person, Leonard. Leonard was wearing a big white bib that he was drooling on. Lee looked at Leonard dribbling on his bib and said, "Let's go, Nancy, there's no way we can get through to this person." Nancy replied, "C'mon, Lee. He's a fellow human being, too, isn't he?" Then she placed a funny balloon hat on his head. Lee took one of his little red hearts and placed it on Leonard's bib. He took a deep breath, leaned down and gave Leonard a hug.

All of a sudden Leonard began to squeal, "Eeeeehh! Eeeeeehh!" Some of the other patients in the room began to clang things together. Lee turned to the staff for some sort of explanation only to find that every doctor, nurse and orderly was crying. Lee asked the head nurse, "What's going on?"

Lee will never forget what she said: "This is the first time in 23 years we've ever seen Leonard smile."

How simple it is to make a difference in the lives of others.

– Jack Canfield and Mark V. Hanson

Chicken Soup For The Soul

MAKE HUGGING A HABIT

You and I can make a difference by reaching out to hug at least twelve people every day, looking into their eyes and telling them that they really do matter.

Love is only love if it is given, and must be given away to be received. People do not care how much you know until they know how much you care. Giving every person you meet a warm smile is another beautiful way to express your love.

My twelve year old daughter Krystal expresses her love to me by writing the sweetest love notes and leaving them on my dresser. I find them when I am tying my tie in the mornings. My children call me at my office every day to tell me they love me. They ask me what time I am coming home and finish the conversation by asking, "Daddy, are you staying home tonight?"

Flowers are also a great way to show your love and appreciation to someone. On Valentines Day four years ago, I brought home a dozen roses for my wife, as I do on occasion. When my daughter Krystal saw her mother's roses she asked me, "Dad, when are you going to start bringing roses home for me?" So two weeks later I brought home eight roses for her eighth birthday and she was thrilled. Here is the note she wrote to me that night and I found stuck to my mirror the next morning as I was dressing:

Dear: Dad, I Love YOU, and you are one of the greatest dad. I would like to show you this Poem that I wrote!

Thanksgiving

I am thankful for a house
That is very warm inside,
I like my big room
That is very big and wide.
I am thankful for my Mom and Dad
Their a great family
Even though we fight at times
We get along happily.
I am thankful for my friends,
They are very nice to me.
We like each other a lot,
They're the nicest they can be.

I am thankful for my food
My mom is a very good cook.
She makes very good food
Without a book. The End

Thank you for the flowers you gave me.
They are beautiful.

Love Krystal

SPEAK WITH LOVE

Speak kindly. As a leader in business, I have found that speaking in a kind, loving (but sometimes firm) voice is the best way to gain respect. The loving words of compliment, praise and reassurance will build the self-esteem of the people around you and you will feel much better yourself in the process. It is amazing when you try catching people doing something right, how many opportunities for praise you find in one day.

Criticism destroys self-esteem. We all know that there has never been a statue erected to a critic. Criticism is like a gift, it belongs to the giver until it is received by the recipient. Before accepting any criticism, be certain it is being given in love. If not, give it back to the person that has given it.

LOVE YOURSELF

Since you're the only person you'll be with all the time for the rest of your life, choose to love yourself.

"Love never fails" — *The Bible*

Hugs

It's wondrous what a hug can do,
A hug can cheer you when you're blue.
A hug can say, "I love you so,"
or "Gee! I Hate to see you go."

A hug is, "Welcome back again!"
or "Where've you been?"
A hug can soothe a small child's pain
And bring a rainbow after rain.

The hug! There's no doubt about it'
We scarcely could survive without it.
A hug delights and warms and charms,
It must be why God gave us arms.

Hugs are great for fathers and mothers,
Sweet for sisters, swell for brothers,
and chances are some favorite aunts
love them more than potted plants.

Kittens crave them. Puppies love them.
Heads of state are not above them.
A hug can break the language barrier,
And make the dullest day seem merrier.

No need to fret about the store of 'em.
The more you give, the more there are of 'em.
So stretch those arms without delay
and give someone a hug today.

— Author Unknown

CHAPTER — 17

TIME MANAGEMENT
BY SELF-MANAGEMENT

"I JUST DON'T HAVE ENOUGH TIME."

We have all been known to make that statement at some time or another. But we all have all the time there is. We all have the same twenty-four hours, the same 1440 minutes as everyone else. It doesn't matter if you are Bill Gates or a waitress in the diner down the street, God gave us all the same great equalizer — twenty-four hours in one day. What most people lack is not time - but rather, the skills to manage themselves and the time they have available. High achievers manage their time wisely. They make every minute count.

Time is much like money. When you decide to spend an hour watching TV, you have decided to *not* spend an hour doing everything else. Winners don't spend time, they invest it. They expect a return on every hour they invest, whether it be in their business, their family or their own well being.

YOUR TIME IS YOUR LIFE

When you give away your money, you are giving away something that can be replaced. When you give away your time, you are giving them a part of your life. Thus, time management is life management. Waste your time, and you are wasting your life. There are many renewable resources, but time is not one of them.

Control your time and you are controlling your life. Controlling your time really means controlling the events in your life. People in control of the events in their life are confident, happy, and powerful. They possess one thing above all: *inner peace.*

TIME MANAGEMENT

"Time management" is not a new idea. There has been an entire industry built to serve the person who just can't seem to get organized. Everything from *Daytimers, Things-To-Do-Today* pads, to time management software is available to plan and track personal time usage. Why then is time management or, shall we say life management, such a challenge? You'll only manage your life as well as you manage your time.

As human beings, we tend to blame others for our shortage of time. There are many readily available scapegoats: drop-in visitors, meetings, inadequate equipment, telephone interruptions and one crisis after another. However, the only one to blame is ourselves - for letting our time be wasted. Once again, we cannot manage time; we can only manage ourselves!

TIME MANAGEMENT BY SELF-MANAGEMENT

There is another reason time management is such a challenge: *conditioning.* We've been conditioned to believe that certain things about ourselves and our surroundings are the truth. As a result of conditioning, many people have adopted myths about their lives as being the truth.

Visit a circus, and you will see what I mean about conditioning. Take a look at the elephants tied to little stakes that they could easily pull out, yet those little stakes keep the huge elephants tethered. When the elephants are young, they are chained by the leg to immovable stakes. However, little by little, over the period of a month, the elephants are conditioned to think they can't move about as long as they are tied by the right rear leg. From the moment this conditioning takes effect, you could tie these elephants with a string and they wouldn't move. They don't move about because they *believe* they can't. The tethers in their minds are stronger than any chains.

THE TRUE PURPOSE OF TIME MANAGEMENT

The value of time management is not to control time, since time cannot be controlled, but to use time to improve our lives. Time management will not give us more hours in a day, but it will give us a better life. It can enhance our lives by:

1. *Reducing stress*
2. *Bringing balance into our lives*
3. *Helping us avoid procrastination*
4. *Making us more productive*
5. *Helping us achieve our goals.*

TIME MANAGEMENT = STRESS PREVENTION

Deadlines are a major contributing factor in stress. It is impossible to manage stress without learning to manage our time. In fact, by learning to manage our time, we are learning to prevent stress. The better we learn to manage our time, the more we avoid unnecessary stress and the less we need coping techniques. Why learn to cope with stress if we can learn to prevent the stress that time shortages inflict on us?

If time management equals stress prevention, then time management also prevents illness. Stress is now linked directly to some of our most serious health concerns, heart attacks and strokes being the most common. In the business world, this means two things: the loss of some of the brightest and most promising managers, and the rising cost of company-paid health care plans. Stress-induced disability claims are becoming a major headache, not only for insurance companies, but also for employers who are sued for causing the disability.

BALANCING BETWEEN BUSINESS AND PERSONAL LIFE

Most entrepreneurs are self-motivated people, driven by an unseen force from within to achieve the goals they have set for their lives. Usually, that means the goals they have set for their business. Hence, they see little value in helping their employees achieve a balance in their lives. However, it's not only entrepreneurs who are addicted to work.

The single mother holding down two jobs to make ends meet would not consider herself a workaholic; "she's just doing what she has to do." It's not the long hours, but the reason behind the long hours that make us workaholics.

For the workaholic who just doesn't have enough hours in a day, time management is a simple cure. However, since workaholism is addictive and compulsive behavior, and true workaholics are addicted to work, time management, in itself, is seldom a cure. A new set of values must accompany new time management skills in order to bring a balance to the life of the workaholic.

PROCRASTINATION

Procrastination is the most common self-inflicted time robber. For the salesperson, it's putting off that phone call. For some, it's putting off the beginning of an exercise program. "Putting things off" has probably caused more time management problems than all the other causes put together. We have a natural tendency to do the things we like and put off the things we don't. We need to develop a sense of urgency for each task and remember that time is of the essence.

INCREASED PRODUCTIVITY

A good time management system will certainly improve our productivity. The more productive we are, the greater our advantage over our competition. The reason that today there is so much "downsizing," "restructuring," and "rightsizing" going on in companies really comes down to the issue of productivity. The only way a company or a country can regain its competitive edge is to improve productivity.

What's productivity anyway? Productivity refers to the relationship between results and resources. In other words, productivity equals output divided by input. This formula demonstrates that there are two ways to improve productivity: to hold output constant while reducing input and to increase output without increasing input.

How much can we improve our productivity? While very little research has been done in this area, there is some data available that would indicate that the average manager is only 30% effective. Returning phone calls several at a time can reduce the average time spent per call by 50%. Closing your office door and working without interruption for two hours a day will enable you to accomplish what would have taken you three hours before.

GOAL ACHIEVEMENT

All goals must have a deadline. Without a goal, it doesn't matter how long it takes you to arrive. That reminds me of the story of the little boy who asks his father as he arrives home from work one day, "Daddy, what did you do at work today?' "Oh, not much, son." replies his Dad. "Well then," replies the boy "how did you know when you were finished?"

There many times when one activity can be taking you towards two or more goals at the same time. For instance, if three of your goals were to spend a half an hour a day exercising, half an hour a day in solitude, half an hour a day in prayer, you could achieve all three at once by praying as you jogged or walked alone for a half an hour. Family time and exercise can be combined. I combine travel and charitable work by going on mission trips to foreign countries.

"All time management begins with planning."

– Tom Greening and Dick Hobson

BUILDING A FOUNDATION FOR TIME MANAGEMENT

Set priorities for your goals. *"A major part of successful living lies in the ability to put first things first. Indeed, the reason most major goals are not achieved is that we spend our time doing second things first."*

– Robert J. McKain

Any successful time management system needs to be developed upon a firm foundation - our core values or the highest priorities for our lives. In other words, we need to determine what the *First Things* are in our lives.

BENJAMIN FRANKLIN

No one explains this subject better that Hyrum W. Smith in his book *10 Natural Laws Of Successful Time And Life Management*. Hyrum, who has developed the Franklin Day Planner into a huge business, tells in his book, how Benjamin Franklin, at the age of twenty-two, conceived the "bold and arduous task of arriving at moral perfection." He began the process by asking himself the question: "What are the highest priorities in my life?" as a result of his introspection, he emerged with twelve "virtues" — his governing values, each qualified with a written statement:

Temperance	"Eat not to dullness; drink not to elevation."
Silence	"Speak not but what may benefit others or yourself; avoid trifling conversation."
Order	"Let all things have their places; let each part of your business have its time."
Resolution	"Resolve to perform what you ought; perform without fail what you resolve."
Frugality	"Make no expense but to do good to others or yourself; that is, waste nothing."
Industry	"Lose no time; be always employed in

something useful; cut off all unnecessary actions."

Sincerity "Use no hurtful deceit; think innocently and justly, and, if you speak, speak accordingly."

Justice "Wrong none by doing injuries; or omitting the benefits that are your duty."

Moderation "Avoid extremes; forbear resenting injuries so much as you think they deserve."

Cleanliness "Tolerate no uncleanliness in body, clothes, or habitation."

Tranquillity "Be not disturbed at trifles, or at accidents common or unavoidable."

Chastity "Rarely use venery but for health or offspring, never to dullness, weakness, or the injury of our own or another's peace or reputation."

Franklin took these twelve statements to a Quaker friend of his to get his opinion of them. The Quaker friend informed him that he'd forgotten one: humility. He "kindly inform'd me," said Ben, *"that I was generally thought proud; that my Pride show'd itself frequently in conversation; that I was not content with being in the right when discussing any point, but was rather overbearing and insolent; of which he convinced me by mentioning several instances."*

So Franklin added a thirteenth virtue - *Humility.* He wrote a four-word statement describing what it meant to him: "Imitate Jesus and Socrates." He then organized his life into thirteen week cycles, and for one week out of thirteen, he would mentally focus on one of those virtues in an effort to bring his performance in line with his values.

Franklin wrote in his memoirs at the age of seventy-eight, *"On the whole, tho' I never arrived at the perfection I had been so ambitious of obtaining, but fell far short of it, yet I was by the endeavor a better and a happier man than I otherwise should have been, if I had not attempted it."* However, he adds, when speaking of *Humility, "I cannot boast of much success in acquiring the reality of this virtue; but I had a good deal with regard to the appearance of it."*

First, Ben identified his values; next, he made a concerted effort to live his life according to those values, day in and day out. Even though there existed a gap between his ideals and reality, as there always is, that fact is that: "his performance improved because of his ideals." This improvement is the source of what we all are looking for — inner peace. Abraham Maslow referred to this unity between our values and our everyday performance as "self-actualization." *It is a bringing together of what I do and what I really value.*

IDENTIFYING YOUR VALUES

Everyone has a set of values, but not everyone has identified them. The exercise of examining your life and facing up to your actual values is a challenging but rewarding experience.

James W. Newman, author of *Release Your Brakes!*, developed a scenario to help you reach down inside and discover what your values are.

Imagine, if you will, that I take you to one of my construction sites, and there lying on the ground is an I-Beam 120 ft. long. Now, imagine that I'm standing on one end of the I-Beam, and I ask you to stand on the other end, 120 feet away from me. I reach into my pocket and take out a hundred-dollar bill. I then yell down to you "I'll give you this hundred-dollar bill if walk the length of this beam in less than two minutes without falling off either side." Would you take the walk? Of course, you would.

Now, suppose this same I-Beam were taken to New York City and lifted 1,360 feet above the ground and used as a bridge between the two buildings called the World Trade Center. A very narrow bridge. Only twelve inches wide. If I now stood on one building and you stood on the other, would you now cross the beam for a hundred-dollar bill. Not a chance! Would you do for a hundred thousand dollars? Not likely! Why not? Because you value your life more than the money.

Now, let's suppose I'm holding your child on the other end of the beam. I now holler across to you "If you don't come across the beam right now, I'll drop your child." Would you now risk the crossing? If so, you obviously value your child's safety more than your own. The question is, *"If we value the lives of our kids enough to die for them, why don't we value their lives enough to live for them?"*

We all have governing values, and thanks to Hyrum W. Smith, I have taken the time to identify mine. What a rewarding exercise! I challenge you to stop reading right now, and spend the 4-8 hours it will take to complete your own personal constitution.

I'm going to share with you my governing values to give you an example of what I am talking about. In some of these areas, I have not yet arrived. However, my architect (God) and I have completed the ideal design. He's just not done working on me yet. God must visualize a "finished" Ben Kubassek as He keeps working on me, and so I do the same as I review my values.

1. *I serve God with a passion.* I have a relationship with my Creator. I'm not religious. I'm a spiritual being with a physical body. Whenever I doubt the existence

of a God, I look at a tree, or a flower, or look up the stars, or think about the birth of one my children. He's been so good to me.

2. *I'm a blessing to every person I meet.* Every morning during my quiet time, I ask God to make me a blessing to everyone I will meet that day. My desire is to have people feel better about themselves because of their encounter with me. I love to encourage and inspire people to reach their full potential.

3. *I am a great husband and father.* I make time for my family, helping them spiritually, financially, physically and intellectually. I also make time, just to play with them. I build the self-esteem of my children by encouraging them and praising them. I make only positive statements in their presence.

4. *I am constantly building my mind.* I never stop learning. I read books, listen to tapes, and watch positive TV programs that will make me more intelligent, expand my vocabulary, improve my business skills, and enhance my people skills.

5. *I maintain a sound mind and a healthy body.* I eat healthy and never to excess. I exercise regularly and get adequate sleep in order to maintain a high level of energy. I guard myself against negative thoughts and negative people.

6. *I spend time alone every day.* The first hour of my day, I spend in solitude. I spend this time in prayer and start planning my day. This power hour sets the stage for my entire day. It is the first step towards inner peace.

7. *I have order in my life.* My person, home and office are clean, tidy and organized. I dress up and try to look my best, even if I'm not feeling my best.

8. *I have Wisdom that comes from above.* I start every

day with a prayer for God's wisdom to fill me for the day! Wisdom is the skillful application of knowledge. God's wisdom enables me to use the knowledge and experience I've gathered to glorify Him.

9. *I'm a generous person.* I'm a giver. I give with much joy, my love, money and time, helping those in need. I give expecting to receive a blessing from above. However, I never give expecting something in return from the person I am helping. Thank you Lord for parents who taught me the joy of giving!

10. *I am financially secure.* I have developed an income that is residual. It is there whether I'm capable of working or not. My family's needs for food, clothing, shelter and education are adequately met.

11. *I'm productive and effective.* I manage my time and do first things first. I make things happen. For me, time is always of the essence.

12. *I'm persistent in achieving the goals I've set.* I never, ever, ever give up. I may change direction, but I never stop moving.

13. *I am quick to forgive others.* My memory is good except when it comes to remembering how others have hurt me in word or deed.

14. *I honor my father and mother.* I thank God for wonderful Christian parents who taught me the meaning of cheerful giving and that "what I was, was God's gift to me; what I would become, would be my gift to God."

15. *I live my life with an attitude of gratitude.* I am thankful for all the good things my life has been blessed with: my family, my friends, a healthy body, my energy, a creative mind, and the list goes on.

ABUNDANT LIVING IS MEANT TO BE OURS, HERE AND NOW!

Guilt, worry, and a lack of a sense of accomplishment are feelings to get rid of before laying your head on your pillow. Before retiring to bed each night, stand in front of a mirror, look yourself in the eye and repeat the following affirmation:

"I _____ am an honest person of integrity with self-discipline and a high self- esteem. I am a forgiving, loving, caring individual. I have faith, hope for the future and vision. I am enthusiastic, energetic and take pride in everything I do. I have wisdom and a sense of humor. I make a difference wherever I am. I have a passion for excellence. I am loyal, trustworthy, dependable and have character. I inspire people with my charisma and strong convictions."

"I am optimistic, positive and intelligent. I am a high-achiever with a balanced life. I serve mankind by meeting human needs. I am firm but sensitive and fair. I am self-confident and bold yet humble. I have class. I love my family and people in general. I'm a hugger. I am fun-loving, health conscious and creative. I am highly effective, punctual and manage my time well. I have written, balanced goals for my life. I'm a winner."

"I was created to achieve my full potential. I will strive to be the best I can possibly be."

CHAPTER — 18

*F*AILURE ISN'T A PERSON...
IT'S ONLY AN EVENT

Persistence and faith are the keys to unlocking the door between you and what you desire in life. Giving up will mean living the rest of your life in the shadows of defeat. Winning in the end makes you and others forget about your past failures.

The exciting news is that every successful person has experienced failure. Henry Ford said, *"Whew! I'm glad to have known failure. Now I can know success!"*

People with low self-esteem have great difficulty in accepting the responsibility for their failures. They are unhappy with their performance and feel better if they can put the blame on someone else. Why not just forgive and accept ourselves?

I'm not ashamed to admit that I've failed more than most people I know. I've also succeeded more than most people I know. The best way to handle failure is honestly and positively. Every failure means you had the guts to start. Failure reminds you that you're human.

When people fail at one thing, they try to connect the present failure with a previous failure. They then make the assumption that they are not very good at anything.

Faith is always more powerful than failure. With faith in yourself and the God that created you, you can begin again. With faith, there comes hope; with hope, we never give up. These people refused to give up:

- Thomas Edison was thrown out of school in the early grades when teachers decided he couldn't do the work.
- W. Clement Stone, successful insurance company executive and founder of Success magazine, was a high school dropout.
- R.H. Macy failed seven times before his store in New York caught on.
- Novelist John Creasey got 753 rejection slips before he published the first of his 564 books.

The thing all winners have in common is that they don't quit in the face of adversity or setback. They just get back up when they are knocked down; they just keep doin' it and doin' it and doin' it.

FAILING FORWARD

I'd like to share with you the success principles I've learned from my failures. And, since everything we learn is a result of our own failures or someone else's failures, I'll also be sharing with you the most significant failure, one that was not my own, but one that affected my life greatly and one that I learned a wealth of wisdom from.

The key is to learn from our old mistakes so that we can make new ones. A book about succeeding would not be complete without a chapter on failing.

I now reflect back on burnout as *"my best/worst experience."* Let me tell you why I have mixed feelings. I guess you could say I have mixed feelings because I went over the edge of a cliff and into the depths of depression and despair but, in the process I became a more caring, compassionate person who could help others going through the same experience. You can't say *"I know where you're coming from"* if you've never been there!

My burnout was a result of failure in three areas of my life: physically, mentally and spiritually. These failures would teach me more than all my successes combined.

Physical Failure - As my business grew and it consumed more of my waking hours, the less time I took for physical exercise. Sitting behind my desk, my body was soon so out of shape that my mind decided to follow.

Mental Failure - The busier I got at the office, the less time I took to spent in solitude, reading books and listening to motivational tapes as I was driving. My mind became a vacuum that soon filled with the ghosts of worry, fear and anxiety. It was once a mind that used to be filled with positive thoughts and dreams.

Spiritual Failure - As my life reached warp speed, I began to spend less time alone, talking to my Creator and building the relationship that I had with Him. My life began to lose its purpose as I lost the vision I once had. I became depressed and even contemplated taking my life.

What did I learn from my failures leading to burnout?

1. I learned to balance my life by setting realistic goals in all areas of my life. Family goals, financial goals, mental goals, spiritual goals, physical goals, and social goals. I learned to set short-term, mid-term, and long-term goals in all those areas.

2. I learned that you can have balance without success (that's have nothin', do nothin', and be nothin'), but, you can't have true success without balance.

3. I have learned to spend time alone every morning while I exercise and keep my body fit.

4. I have learned to regularly feed my mind with the best books, tapes, and programming I can find such as The Peoples Network.

5. I learned to dream again. More importantly, I began to include others in my dreams. Within 3 years after my burnout, my wife Elizabeth and I traveled to the country of Guatemala to see some projects that an organization by the name of Missionary Ventures International (MVI) was involved with. MVI is a non-profit, non-denominational mission whose goal is meeting human needs through personal involvement. As a result of the impact of that first visit, I came back to Canada and decided that we needed an MVI Canada. As a result of sharing that idea, people in this area have helped build 10 schools in Guatemala, now over 3,000 Guatemalan kids go to these schools every day, 3,000 kids who have a better chance at doing something with their lives. A hospital has been com pleted with the help of local people. In Romania, we helped clothe kids abandoned in the AIDS hospital in Constanta, local people donated hundreds of Teddy Bears, fellow Canadians helped Romanians in Basarabi renovate a derelict apartment building into a church, and we have fed and clothed the starving

Gypsy kids on the streets. All because I started to dream again. These dreams were bigger than myself; they included others.

The second major failure that I'd like to tell you about, is also the most recent in my life — financial failure. It was not nearly as painful and devastating as burnout but, like burnout, it was a learning experience!

Is it easy to share with you the details of my financial failure? No easier than it was for me to share the details of my experience after I went through burnout! But sharing that experience has helped many people beat depression and live again; it's given burnout victims hope; it has literally saved lives! Likewise, I believe that if you listen carefully, you'll learn lessons from my financial failure that will put money in the bank for you.

Every effect has a cause. Just as my burnout experience was caused by physical, mental, and spiritual failure on my part. My financial failure was caused by failure to focus, and failure to control.

The first cause of my financial failure was a lack of focus. In the mid to late eighties, things were booming in the Home Building Industry. It was easy to get the sale. It was hard to get the trades. The secret, I felt at the time, would be a vertically integrated home-building business, a company that would control everything from servicing the lot to installing the kitchen cabinets. Before you knew it, I had twelve companies and seventy-five employees, some-days working on as many as twenty different projects at the same time. Many job sites, I never even got to see.

Besides running all those companies, I was a director on the board of Teen Challenge Canada, President of the K-W Homebuilder's Association, and President of Missionary Ventures Canada. I had learned to balance but, I had not learned how to focus.

CASH CRUNCH

The second cause of financial failure was the failure to control. Mr. Lyle Hallman, local builder, landlord, and one of my mentors, gave me some good advice a few years ago. It was this: "Ben, you will learn one thing in business: nobody looks after your money like you do." Being out of control is the greatest cause of stress there is. My group of companies were like a monster spinning out of control. The only way to stop the momentum, was to throw a monkey wrench in the spokes.

As margins got tighter and as sales were off by 40% for us in 1995, as it was on average across the board in the province of Ontario, cashflow became a monumental challenge. My Controller told me he was spending half of his week talking to suppliers and the other half monitoring cash flow, both of which I now do in less than twenty minutes a day, by the way, because I am now my own controller.

We were fortunate, or so we thought at the time, to have a large lumber supplier give us extended terms on our lumber purchases in exchange for exclusivity. That was until October 1995, when this supplier decided they needed their cash more than we did. We agreed to do our best to bring our account current by the end of the year and paid off $300,000 in 45 days. However, financing that was promised didn't materialize and a payment on account was missed. Our friendly supplier was no longer friendly.

On January 15, 1996 this supplier threatened to slap a general lien across all our projects if they were not paid forthwith for all lumber purchases up to the previous day. A general lien in this situation would be very illegal but very effective in shutting down our operations. This supplier had done this before and we couldn't say we weren't warned well in advance to beware. After meeting with our banks, we made a proposal to pay off the entire account from finance draws and closings over the next 60 days. No deal! The supplier filed its lien and chaos was the best way to describe the month that followed.

What my controller had failed to tell me was that he hadn't controlled my bank accounts. He had run them over 6 figures into overdraft. I found that out on January 05, 1996 when I received a call from my banker. Talk about out of control! To take control of the company I went from being merely the CEO to being CEO, CFO, and COO all within a month. As I nearly doubled the number of hours I worked in a week, I was able to test the Principles Of Balance I had been writing about for the past five years. Could I work like a workaholic without becoming one? The answer is yes.

Here are the lessons I learned going through financial failure:

1. **I learned to narrow my focus.** Our company's only focus at this time is creating residential communities, while sub-contracting everything from the plumbing to bookkeeping. In business and in life, it takes focus on a goal to maintain the correct heading or direction.

   I like the story about the guy from the city driving by this farm and seeing all these bullseyes painted on the one side of the barn with an arrow dead center in each one. He decides to stop and meet this fantastic marksmen. He pulls up the driveway and there is the farmer sitting on the porch. He says, "Sir, how is that you hit the bull's eye with everyone of those arrows. "It's easy," the farmer said "I shoot the arrow first and paint the bull's eye later." To be successful in business you must paint the bull's eye first.

2. **I learned to never give up control.** In January 1997 of this year I began a painful downsizing to the point where I once again had control. To go from seventy-five employees to seven means telling some people that their services are no longer required. Most of those people still provide their services to me, but I'm now their customer instead of their employer. Is that good or is that good?

    For the past nine months I have signed every piece of paper going in and out of our companies. We have sold & built more homes in eight months this year with the few employees we have, than in twelve months last year with all the previous staff. Within a month the two companies of mine that were forced into receivership by the illegal actions of one large supplier will be out of receivership and back in my control.

3. **I learned to ask for help when I need it.** Do you know why it takes 50,000 sperm cells to fertilize one egg? Because they are just like men, they won't stop to ask directions. Ask for help when you need it. Despite what you have heard about the ruthless actions of banks, I can tell you nothing but good things about the actions of our banks when I went to ask them for help in a crisis. They actually increased our line of credit to give us some much needed breathing space.

4. **I learned to never quit.** Most people give up on the brink of a miracle. It may be the ninth inning and you are down by three runs. Don't give up. You can win it with one swing of the bat. After seven months of fighting every day to get a judge to hear our case, it was finally heard and the illegal lien was removed from all our projects. Don't ever quit. Hang in there.

JUST LIKE DAD

Isn't it wonderful kids want to be just like there dads! Or is it?

I'll never forget the day five years ago, my oldest son Daniel was six and it was time for his annual summer buzz-cut. Now, I always cut my boys hair for two reasons: I get to spend time one-on-one with them and, second, it's tremendous sense of being in control when you are holding that buzzing hair clipper. The worst sound you can hear, during a hair cut is "Whoops". So, Daniel is sitting there as I am getting the clippers oiled, and he looks up at me with his big brown eyes and says, "Daddy, I want my hair cut just like yours." I asked "Son, how's that?" He said "You know Daddy, just like yours. The front, I want it cut into a letter "M".

As I began to study the lives of those people I considered successful, I realized that most men that were successful financially, were failures as fathers. They had little time for their kids, didn't hug them or kiss them, or tell them that they loved them and that they were proud of them. I decided to learn from their failures;

- I tell my kids that I'm proud of them.
- I tell them they have greatness within them. That they can do anything, have anything, or be anything they want to be.
- I hug and kiss my kids every day.
- At night when I tuck them in, I kneel down at the side of each of their beds, I press my cheek against theirs, I tell them I'm proud to be their dad, I say a blessing over them, listen to their prayers, kiss them good night, hug them, and I tell them that I love them.
- I eat breakfast and most dinners with my family.

I hope that by sharing with you my failures, you will be inspired to move;

- **From failure to fight.** Don't ever quit. I 'd rather fail doing something I love, than succeed at doing something I hate. Don't let others rain on your parade, just because they don't have a parade of their own.
- **From burnout to balance.** Keep first things first. Even if you've never done it before, go and hug your son or your daughter, tell them you're sorry where you've failed as a dad. Tell them that you love them.
- **From success to significance.** Be bold enough to make a difference. Get involved in your church and your community. Go on a mission trip.
- **And from living to legacy.** Leave a path for your kids to follow. Dads, remember this: Kids start pouring dope into their veins when their dads stop pouring hope into their dreams.

Last of all, don't ever give up! Don't ever quit! You could be giving up on the brink of a miracle.

FAILURE

You may have a fresh

start

any moment you

choose,

for this thing we call

"FAILURE"

is not the falling down,

but the staying down.

CHAPTER — 19

SURVIVING SUCCESS – HOW TO KEEP FROM HITTING THE BOTTOM AFTER YOU'VE MADE IT TO THE TOP

MANY PEOPLE DISCOVER that the cost of success is too great. They expected to make some sacrifices on their way to the top with the hope that, when they reached the peak, they would be rewarded with a big pay-off.

What the rich and powerful discover when they reach the top and have reaped the material rewards is that they have been emotionally swindled in the process. The isolation that comes with success is something few are prepared for. I can tell you from experience, that as you reach the heights of achievement and success financially, you will also reach new depths of loneliness, unless you are psychologically prepared. Invitations to the homes of your friends, even those who visit yours regularly, are now a rare occurrence at best. As a result, highly successful people often have an overwhelming sense of emptiness and isolation. They are also prone to severe bouts of depression at times.

THE PEDESTAL SYNDROME

When a person achieves success in one area of life, that person is placed on a pedestal in the minds of his/her peers. She/he is presumed to be talented and competent in all other areas as well. These high expectations are often more than we are equipped to live up to.

However, the rewards are many, and the key to enjoying an abundant life at the top is that thing called *Balance*. It helps to view our lives as a scale of justice with multiple arms, each representing the following areas of our lives:

1. **Spiritual.** In my study of highly successful people, those who stay healthy when they reach the top have a strong religious involvement. The church is a vital part of their lives. The shaping of their character began with the training they received as a child — training in attitude, work ethic and moral standards. The spiritual arm of your scale should contain the following elements:

    • Church attendance and involvement.

    • Daily solitude, prayer and reading.

    • Giving of your time and talents to the nurturing of others.

2. **Recreational.** Without our playtime, life can get pretty boring. Recreation is the best antidote for the stress we experience in our quest for the summit. It is as vital to living a balanced life as the air we breathe.

With recreation as a priority in our lives, we are less likely to overextend ourselves to our careers or businesses. Our recreational side includes the following:

- Personal hobbies.
- Taking your children to sports, lessons and other activities.
- Going for a walk with your family on Sunday afternoons.
- Vacations.

3. **Financial.** Without an eye continually on this side of the balance, the super-achiever becomes a workaholic, the giver becomes greedy and money becomes the god we serve. Our financial arm needs to be balanced with:

- Earning.
- Saving.
- Giving.

THE PRINCIPLE OF BALANCE

In order to maintain balance in our lives, we need to maintain an equal weight (representing the energy we expend) on each of the arms of our scale of justice. If we increase the number of hours we work in a week, we need to increase our recreational time by the same percentage. At the same time we need to increase the amount of time we spend in solitude. If the amount we earn increases, so should the amount we give and save.

Tallying the weight on each arm is a continual exercise but will ensure that we always maintain a balance in our lives. With balance in our lives, we become a blessing. We become a blessing to our family...a blessing to a world less fortunate ... and a blessing to every person we meet.

A boxer knows the importance of balance when fighting in the ring. Caught off balance, a boxer is easily flattened by his opponent. Without balance, the blows that life deals us from time to time will knock us off of our feet. When we're in balance ... we simply fight back. When we've been punched, we bounce right back like a punching bag.

A cheque book needs to be balanced monthly to verify all the credits and debits. The purpose of balancing our chequing account is to make certain our outgo does not exceed our income and that our upkeep does not become our downfall. So too do our lives need to be balanced on a regular basis. It's not a one-time exercise, but an ongoing process.

Like a tight-rope walker without a balance pole, you will find it impossible to successfully walk the tight-rope of life. Without a grasp of the laws of balance as your balance pole, you will be in danger of falling.

Life can be balanced bliss, blessed with abundance and filled with peace and true happiness when you take the principles in this book and make them your own formula for balanced success. These are all universal, timeless operating laws that work, whether or not we believe in them. These principles are like the law of gravity. Whether or not you believe in it, if you jump out a plane at 5000 ft. without a parachute, you're going to hit the ground pretty hard. By learning and internalizing these principles, we are able to make them work for us so that we reach the full potential intended for every area of our lives.

"Achieving our full potential is the process of becoming all that we can. Success is not only the happiness we experience when we reach our destination; it's also the joy that comes with the journey."

HELICOPTER TRAINING

"You've got the controls." It's the voice of my flight instructor in my headset. Learning to fly a helicopter is not impossible — it just seemed that way to me. It's Day - One of flight training for my Private Helicopter License. As my instructor put us into a perfect, motionless hover (using all your skill to go exactly nowhere), I realized how important balance is when it comes to keeping this machine right-side up.

For an ecstatic couple of seconds, I think I'm in control. After all, I'm already one hour into my first lesson. How difficult can it possibly be to keep this little egg-beater upright?

Then the hover begins to decay and saucer. We drift from side to side, pitching and rolling, lurching forward, sliding back, rising and falling like a hat in the wind. Every correction I make only amplifies my next mistake. After a couple of seconds, I hear his calm voice in the head-set — "I've got it." Almost before he finishes speaking, we become level and motionless and poised for whatever he wants to do next. "It's the sense of balance you're missing," he says "you need to imagine you are balancing yourself on top of a beach ball." I now have a new appreciation for the word balance. To maintain balance in life is much like maintaining *balance* in a helicopter, it requires small adjustments as you begin to feel the shifts in balance, long before you are able to see them.

Remember to always stay in touch with yourself, sensing any shift in balance. Apply the principles of balance and you will survive, learn, and grow. You will become a new creature, one that has risen above burnout.

Ben's Recommended Food For The Mind:

1. Bland, Glenn — *Success! The Glenn Bland Method.* Tyndale House Publishers Inc. 1972

2. Canfield, Jack and Hanson, Mark Victor — *Chicken Soup for the Soul.* Health Communications Inc. 1993

3. Conwell, Russell H. — *Acres of Diamonds.* Harper & Row. 1915

4. Covey, Stephen R. — *The 7 Habits Of Highly Effective People.* Simon & Schuster. 1989 & First Things First Simon & Schuster. 1994

5. Daniels, Peter J. — *How To Be Happy Though Rich.* 1984

6. Hanson, Mark Victor — *Dare To Win.* 1988

7. Hanson, Peter G. — *The Joy Of Stress.* 1985

8. Lee, Larry - Wisdom, *Don't Live Life Without it.* Thomas Nelson Publishers; 1990

9. Mandino, Og — *The Greatest Salesman In The World.* New York; Bantam, 1974 & The Greatest Secrets Of Success.-Video

10. Peal, Norman Vincent — *The Power of Positive Thinking.* Prentice Hall Inc. 1983

11. Schuller, Robert H. — *Tough Times Never Last, But Tough People Do!* Bantam, 1984

12. *The N. I. V. Study Bible* (New International Version). A must for everyday reading in order to live a happy, successful life.

13. Waitley, Denis — *Being The Best.* Oliver-Nelson. 1987

14. Ziglar, Zig — *See You at the Top & Raising Positive Kids in a Negative World.* Thomas Nelson Publishers. 1985

15. Mackenzie Alec, — *The Time Trap.* 1990

16. Smith, Hyrum W. — *The 10 Natural Laws of Successful Time And Life Management.* Warner Books 1994

17. Carnegie, Dale — *How To Stop Worrying and Start Living.* Simon and Shuster. 1984

18. Tracy, Brian — *The Psychology of Achievement.* Audio

19. Rohn, Jim — *The Seasons of Life & Cultivating an Unshakable Character.* Audio

20. Brown, Les — *It's Possible.* Audio

21. Olsen, Jeff & Worre, Eric — *The Peoples Network* — The only network dedicated solely to positive self-help programming.

22. Meyer, Paul J. — *BUILDING FINANCIAL SUCCESS.* Audio

23. Qubein, Nido R.— *Stairway To Success.* Executive Books. 1996.

24. Rodger,-John & McWilliams, Peter — *You Can't Afford The Luxury of a Negative Thought.* Prelude Press. 1991.

25. Chilton, David — *The Wealthy Barber.* Stoddart Publishing Co. Limited. 1989.

26. Harrison, Bob — *POWER POINTS for Success.* Honor Books. 1997

27. McGinnis, Alan Loy — *The BALANCED LIFE.* Augsburg Fortress. 1997

If you can't find *SUCCEED WITHOUT BURNOUT* where you shop, ask your retailer to give us a call. Meanwhile we offer a mail order service for your convienence.

Mail Order Coupon

Please rush me _____ copies of *SUCCEED WITHOUT BURNOUT* at \$15.95 each, including shipping and handling. I have enclosed a cheque made payable to EAGLE PRESS in the amount of \$_____

Full Name:_____

Address:_____

City:_____

Prov./State: _____

Postal/Zip Code: _____

Telephone#:_____ Fax #:_____

For orders of two or more books, discounts apply. Please call or write for volume discount details and information on seminars and keynote speeches.

EAGLE PRESS R.R.#1,
Ayr, Ontario, Canada N0B 1E0
Telephone: 1-800-801-7264 Fax: (519) 740-1008
EMAIL: kubassek@golden.net
WEB PAGE: www.burnout.net

Do you know someone that could benefit from reading *SUCCEED WITHOUT BURNOUT?* It's the perfect gift for everyone from the harried executive to the working mom....a gift that could literally change a life! We'll ship books directly to recepients of your choice if you give us their names and addresses. Attach a personal note or card with your order form and we'll include it in their package.